ART AND HISTORY
OF
SICILY

280 Colour illustrations

BONECHI

Printed in Italy by Centro Stampa Editoriale Bonechi

Text by: Giuliano Valdes, Editing Studio-Pisa

Translated by: Rowena Hill for TRADU.CO s.n.c., Florence

CREDITS

Photographs from the Archives of Casa Editrice Bonechi, taken by :
Marco Banti: pages 54; 105; 106; 108; 109; 130; 131; 132; 133; 134; 135; 136; 143 below;157 above left; 160; 168; 169.

Paolo Giambone: pages 10; 33 above; 35 above; 43; 55; 56; 57; 61; 62-63; 64; 65; 66 above; 67; 73; 74; 75; 76; 77; 78; 79; 80; 81; 82; 86; 89; 90; 91; 93; 97; 98; 99; 114; 115; 118 above; 128; 129.

Giuliano Valsecchi: pages 59; 60; 68; 69; 70; 72; 83; 84; 88; 92 above left; 94-95-96; 100 below; 101; 102; 103; 107 above; 112; 113; 145; 146; 147; 148; 149; 150; 156; 157 above right and below; 158; 159 above; 162; 163; 164.

Other photos:
Gianni Dagli Orti: pages 4; 7; 8 below; 11 above; 19; 20; 21; 22; 23; 24; 25; 26; 27; 30; 31; 32; 36-37-38; 39; 40; 41; 42; 44; 45; 46; 48; 92 below; 100 above; 107 below; 111; 117; 118 below; 119; 120; 121; 122; 123; 124; 125; 126; 127; 137; 139; 141; 142 below; 167 below.

Giovanni Giunta: pages 138; 140; 142 above.

Andrea Pistolesi: pages 11 below; 12; 13; 14; 15; 16; 17; 18; 28; 29.

Foto Tornatore: pages 1; 152-153-154; 159 below; 165.

Giuliano Valsecchi: pages 9; 33 below; 34; 35 below; 47; 49; 50 below; 51; 52; 58; 72 above; 110; 143 above; 144; 151 below; 155; 161; 172 above.

Aerial photographs: I-BUGA: Aut. SMA n. 506-85 pages 6; 166; 171 above. Aut. SMA n. 371-84 pages 8 above; 50 above; 53; 66 below; 71 below; 151 above; 167 above; 170; 171 below; 172 below. Aut. SMA n. 850-86 page 85.

ISBN 88-7009-697-1

*   *   *

INTRODUCTION

HISTORY

A ncient rock engravings have been found which seem to support the theory that the island of Sicily was joined, in the remote past, to the European continent. There are traces of Neolithic settlements, villages built of stone or on palafittes. The early inhabitants of the island included the Sicanians, who were of Iberian origin; they were followed by the Sicels, who came from various regions in southern Italy. When the first Phoenician colony was founded, there were already permanently settled areas on the island; new centres were created at Motye, Trapani, Mazara, Lilybaeum, Palermo and Solunto, and a fertile cultural and commercial interchange started up. We have information on Greek colonies founded in Sicily as early as the eighth century B.C. This region was the most prolific in settlements in the whole territory of Magna Grecia. Greek colonies rose in rapid succession at Naxos, Catania, Leontini, Himera, Messina, Mylae, Syracuse, Megara, Gela and Agrigentum, to mention the largest and most important. In the first half of the fifth century B.C. the first large-scale war in the Mediterranean basin pitted the Syracusans against the Carthaginians, whom they defeated at Himera. The Carthaginians won back and subjected large portions of the island at the end of that century and the beginning of the next. Sicily was finally colonized by the Romans at the end of their recurring wars with Carthage, after a long and tiring campaign. Not until the time of Augustus was the city granted the status of civitas romana, too late to remedy the depredations of his predecessors.

The fall of the Roman Empire was followed by a rapidly changing succession of barbarian peoples (Vandals, Heruli, Goths), until the coming of the Byzantines led by Belisarius. From the ninth to the eleventh century, under the Arabs, Sicily became a Muslim territory; the Arabs left their mark on the way of life, dialectal expressions, placenames and agriculture of the island, turning it into a rich and flourishing land and making Palermo one of the most important cities in Europe.

In the second half of the eleventh century the Arabs were replaced by the Normans, who brought brilliance and luxury to the court of Palermo, promoting the artistic, economic and social development of the city. This period of prosperity continued into the reign of Frederick II of Swabia (first half of the thirteenth century), but came to an end under his successors (his son Manfred was defeated by the Angevins at Benevento in 1266). This was the starting point for the events leading up to the Sicilian Vespers, which chased the French out of the island in 1282. The Aragonese came next, as a prelude to Sicily becoming a Spanish satellite; it became a colony of the Spanish crown until the first half of the eighteenth century.

After that time, as a pawn in the tense game being played out on the chessboard of Europe, Sicily belonged first to the house of Savoy, then to the Austrians and finally (1815) fell into the hands of the Bourbons. Repeated attempts at rebellion culminated in Garibaldi's campaign of 1860 and led to the annexation of Sicily to the new Kingdom of Italy (1861). Problems with their roots far back in the past, backwardness and centuries-old obsessions motivated recurrent insurrections against the great estates and the exploitation of the people by the barons, while lack of confidence in the state, alienation, unemployment and emigration increased. The Fascist government was unable to satisfy the just aspirations of the Sicilians, and after suffering devastation during the war, they felt betrayed and began to threaten partition; their protests were backed by increasing bandit activity (the name of Salvatore Giuliano is known to all). The central government responded by granting Sicily a special 'Statute', which today is still far from having solved the problems of Sicilian society, racked by the recurring spectre of Mafia terrorism and by unassuaged hopes for independence.

ART HISTORY

T he first works of art produced in Sicily go back to prehistoric times. Graffiti and rock paintings have been found at the **Grotte dell'Addaura (Palermo)**, in the **Grotta di S. Teodoro (Messina)** and in caves at **Cala del Genovese (Levanzo)**. During the Neolithic period, while the first indigenous cultures (Stentinello, Lipari), of which many vestiges remain in ceramic and terracotta objects, were developing, relationships with the earliest forms of Aegean culture emerging in the Mediterranean basin were also increasing. The arrival of the Sicels, who imposed their culture on those already existing, was a prelude to the first influx of Phoenicians, around the eleventh century B.C., when the first colonies were founded at Palermo, Solunto and Motye.

From the eighth century B.C. on it was the turn of the Greeks, who settled on the island in several waves, leaving splendid examples of their art, which have come down to us today partly destroyed but still expressive and magnificent. As far as architecture is concerned, we have only to think of the Theatre of Syracuse, certainly the most important of the many in Sicily, the majestic **Temples of Agrigento and Selinunte**, the **Temple of Segesta**, the **Euryalus Castle in Syracuse** and numberless remains of ancient residences, necropolises and burial grounds. The island's museums offer rich glimpses of the painting (painted ceramics and amphoras) and sculpture; we have only to recall the marble Ephebus in the Agrigento Museum, the sculptures and metopes of the temples of Selinunte and bronzes and other carved ornaments of temple buildings.

There are examples of the architectural heritage of the Roman colony at **Catania (Theatre, Amphitheatre)**, **Syracuse (Amphitheatre)**, **Palermo** (remains of houses at **Villa Bonanno**) and **Taormina** (reconstruction of the **Greek Theatre** and **Naumachia**). The exceptional series of mosaics in the **Villa Casale (Piazza Armerina)** is the most important work of decorative art, while Roman sculptures mostly inspired by Classical Greek models can be seen in the museums.

In the Norman period we find an extraordinary flowering of art, uniting and carrying to their highest level of splendour the trends of separate styles previously used by the Byzantines (to transform temples into Christian basilicas) and Arabs (to construct palaces, residences and religious buildings with typically Oriental stylistic characteristics.) Within this sphere we find, in Palermo, the splendid **Cathedral**, the churches of the **Martorana** and **San Giovanni degli Eremiti** (which shows marked Arab influence), the **palaces of La Cuba and La Zisa**, and the **Norman Palace** with the **Palatine Chapel**. In the **Palatine Chapel** and in the **Cathedrals of Cefalù** and **Monreale**, the fantastic, glowing tissue of mosaics achieves an incomparable virtuosity of style.

The buildings of the Gothic period in Sicily are principally defensive. We will mention only the **Castello Ursino** at Catania and the **Castello Maniace** at Syracuse. Catalan influences pentrated from Spain and left an indelible imprint in the Flamboyant Gothic elements commonly found in the decoration of palaces and churches, with a profusion of portals, windows and ornamental features. At the same time the private building activity of the great noble houses was developing and producing powerful and stylistically perfect fortified dwellings. An outstanding example is the Chiaramonte family, whose influential style, called after them 'Chiaramontana', is embodied in the numerous Steri.

Between the fifteenth and sixteenth centuries Sicily produced, in the genius of the painter Antonello da Messina, one of the most brilliant manifestations of the European painting of the time. Other painters we should mention include the De Salibas and Iacobello da Messina. In the field of sculpture, we have the Renaissance artists of the Gagini family, Domenico, the founder, and his sons Antonello and Antonuzzo. Their unmistakable style can be observed all over Sicily in the decoration of churches and basilicas, in a profusion of figures, arches and finely chiselled bas-reliefs. Another outstanding figure in the sculpture of the period is Francesco Laurana.

The Baroque style found in Sicily (seventeenth-eighteenth centuries) one of its most complete expressions, and one with such distinctive features that it is called by the name of Sicilian Baroque. In the context of architecture, building activity flourished in different directions; examples are the churches of the Ragusa region, especially the distinctive churches, both dedicated to **San Giorgio**, built by Gagliardi in Ragusa itself and in Modica, as well as churches in other parts of the island; while Palermo was enhanced by splendid monumental streets and quarters in pure Spanish style. Within the great treasury of Baroque buildings, a distinct strain may be noted at Catania and many minor centres which owe their eighteenth century appearance to massive reconstructions after the earthquake of 1693, largely to be attributed to the architect Vaccarini. In the painting of the time, the influence of the presence in Sicily of famous artists such as Caravaggio and Antonis van Dyck cannot be overlooked.

During the nineteenth century the architecture of the island shows the imprint of Neo-Classicism, which left a considerable number of works at **Palermo (Orto Botanico** and **Teatro Massimo)**, and of Art Nouveau, which was the style of the architect Basile **(Villa Igiea, Villino Florio)**.

TRADITIONS

*I*n Sicily tradition and folklore are two faces of a reality which we can safely call unique and which manifests itself on the occasion of prevalently religious festivities. It is impossible to count, for example, the celebrations that take place all over the island while the church is commemorating **Holy Week**. Other occasions for folk festivities in the Sicilian calendar are the name-days of the numberless patron saints, historical anniversaries and non-religious festivals.

In addition to the colourful island costumes, the **Sicilian Cart** is a unique symbolic item, and at the same time, with its rich painted decorations and ornaments, a natural and genuine expression of its popular culture. So also are the instruments used by the people to make music and accompany an evening's dancing, from the curious 'Jew's harp' (scacciapensieri) to the bagpipes and the tambourine; they are all part of the complex and highly colourful ritual, well typified in the models exhibited in the Pitré Ethnographic Museum in Palermo. Among the traditional art forms, the **Opera dei Pupi** deserves a special mention. Recalling the epic deeds of Orlando and the Paladins, the 'Puppet Opera' is a true theatre of the people, a genuine expression of the culture and history of the island.

Outstanding festivals include the **Epiphany**, celebrated according to the Byzantine and Albanian rites (Mezzojuso, Piana degli Albanesi), the **Festival of St. Sebastian** at Acireale, the spectacular festivals of **St. Agatha**, patron saint of Catania, the **Sagra del Mandorlo in Fiore** at Agrigento, the **Carnival of Acireale**, the **Easter Week** festivities at Caltanissetta, the **Diavolata e Angelicata** at Adrano, the Easter celebrations according to the Byzantine rite at Piana degli Albanesi, the **Ballo dei Diavoli** at Prizzi, the **Festival of St. Vitus** at Mascalucia, the **Festival (Fistinu) of St. Rosalia** at Palermo, the **Luminara di Caltagirone** on the occasion of **the festival** of St. James, the **Palio dei Normanni** at Piazza Armerina, the **Sfilata dei Giganti** at Messina, the **Festival of the Madonna del Ponte** at Caltagirone, the **Procession of St. Lucia** at Syracuse and Belpasso.

Pitré Ethnographical Museum: the Puppet Theatre.

FOOD

*T*he variety and complexity of the culinary art in Sicily is the result of thousands of years of history, the amassing over the centuries of innumerable different layers of civilization and culture. There is, in fact, in almost every dish some ingredient from outside the island; the influences may be Greek, Latin, Arab-Norman, Franco-Hispano-Bourbon. The ancient Greek roots of this cuisine are revealed in simple, natural foods consisting basically of very fresh fish and natural herbs, since special spices and condiments still had to be imported. The Greek cuisine remained true to itself during the time of the Roman occupation, when the island was the 'granary' of the Empire.

The Arabs were responsible for a distinctive trend which to a great extent is at work still today in the food habits of the people of Sicily. They introduced the custom of using Oriental spices in foods, inventing dishes made of 'flour in the shape of threads' (triyah, or the forerunner of modern vermicelli), teaching Sicilians the very famous cuscus, much used in the Trapani region and at Pantelleria, the typical arancine (a sort of derivative of the Arab pilaf, using a lot of saffron). The influence of Arab civilization can be tasted also in the exquisite concoctions of Sicilian cake- and pastry-cooking (a treat for the greedy and an irresistible temptation at every corner). The famous cassata (from the Arab gas at) and torrone (cubayta) are in fact Arab inventions. Refined savourers of seasonal delicacies, the Arabs invented icecream, called 'sorbetto' from the Arab word sharbat. There are endless and surprising combinations, with a decidedly Oriental flavour, using water-melon, pistachio, jasmine (scurzunera), cinnamon, white coffee, almonds.

The Normans, who took over from the Arabs, introduced no substantial changes in culinary habits, which retained their markedly Arab and Oriental character. Game began to be served at this time, while later French influence was responsible for the introduction of the gateau (now more simply called gatto) made of potatoes and rice, other vegetable dishes and the fish soups (madelotte).

It is to the Spanish who ruled Sicily from the fifteenth to the eighteenth century that Sicilians owe the introduction of raw materials and condiments from the New World, as well as typically Spanish food customs. With the importation of peppers, tomatoes, aubergines and potatoes, new tastes were added to the cuisine already existing, giving rise to new blends of foods and combining well chosen ingredients. In the age of the Bourbons it was the turn of the haute cuisine of the nobles and priests.

As well as the dishes already mentioned, the following are typical of Sicilian cuisine: as hors d'oeuvres, stuffed tomatoes, vegetable 'caponata', stuffed or crushed olives; as first course, pasta with sardines, 'pasta 'ncasciata', 'pasta à la Norma', 'crispeddi', 'sfincioni'. As main and side dishes we should mention swordfish 'a ghiotta', aubergines prepared in various ways, sardines 'a beccafico', 'broccoli affogati', 'falsomagro' and a great variety of cheeses, from pecorino to tuma to primosale. From the vast array of sweets and cakes we will mention 'cannoli', 'frutti de Martorana', 'agnello pasquale', 'pignolata' and a great variety of 'granite'. Sicilian wines are of many different kinds and undoubtedly of high quality, pure and strong with a punch in them and often a touch of Marsala quality. As well as the various types of Marsala, we will mention Bianco di Alcamo, Regaleali, Corvo di Salaparuta, various kinds of Moscato and Passito (Pantelleria), the excellent wines of the Etna district (white, rosé and red), Malvasia delle Lipari, Ambrato di Comiso and Faro di Messina.

BATHS

*F*rom the writings of classical Greek authors such as Strabo and Diodorus Siculus, from the many archaeological remains such as the Roman ruins of the Xiphonian Baths (Acireale), from prehistoric vestiges at Termini Imerese and Sciacca and the Roman remains at Terme Vigliatore, the importance of thermal waters in Sicily and their use since immemorial times is immediately clear to us. Baths as an institution and the use of the waters for therapeutic purposes are a tradition many centuries old in Sicily.

Mineral water therapy, inhalation therapy and mud therapy are practised at spas with modern installations. The **Terme Regionali di Acireale** use the waters of St. Venera which are recommended in arthopathy, skin diseases, gynecological problems and diseases of the respiratory tract. The **Terme di Granata Cassibile (Ali Terme)** offer treatment for the sicknesses of childhood, skin diseases, arthropathies, diseases of the respiratory tract and gynecological disorders. The same conditions are treated at the baths of **Germani Marino (Ali Terme)**. At the **Terme Gorga (Calatafimi)** sciatica, rheumatism, skin diseases and disorders of the respiratory tract are treated. The **Terme Segestane (Castellamare del Golfo)** are recommended in metabolic disorders, in arthritis in general, in dermatites and disorders of the respiratory tract. At the **Terme di S. Calogero (Lipari)**, there are treatments for arthrosis, arthropathies, disorders of the metabolism and obesity. The **Terme Regionali di Sciacca** are recommended for a wide range of treatments, which basically include those so far mentioned. The **Bagni di Sclafani (Palermo)** achieve positive results in the treatment of the after-effects of traumas, in polyarthritis and arthrosis, and in skin and related diseases. The **Fonte di Venere Spa (Terme Vigliatore)** is recommended for liver diseases and disorders of the digestive apparatus and the colon, allergic disorders of the respiratory tract, metabolic disorders, dermatites and arthropathies. The **Terme di Termini Imerese** are helpful in the diseases of childhood, inflammations of the respiratory tract, metabolic disorders and arthropathies in general. At the **Terme di Vulcano** positive results are obtained in the treatment of circulatory disorders, rheumatism, arthropathies, neurites and disorders caused by traumas.

PROTECTED AREAS

*I*n the context of environmental protection, Sicily is rapidly falling in line with the decisions of other regions of Italy, respecting what seems to be an inspired international concept for the protection and guardianship of our natural, botanical and zoological heritage.

The **Parco Nazionale dell'Etna** is being set up, while other areas, which in a short time should become the **Parco dei Nebrodi** and the **Parco delle Madonie**, have already been outlined. The Region of Sicily has also passed a law creating numerous protected areas where regulations for the protection of the landscape and natural environment will be applied. Some of the biggest and most important nature reserves are the **Riserva Naturale dei Pantani di Vendicari**, the **Riserva Regionale dell'Isola di Marettimo**, the **Riserva Regionale dello Zingaro**, the **Parco Piano Zucchi**, the **Orto Botanico** and the **Parco della Favorita** and **Parco di Castelnuovo** at Palermo.

Panorama of the city.

A view of the great mass of the main bell tower ▶ of the Cathedral.

PALERMO

Historical Note: A large and important city, Palermo opens like a fan out of its picturesque roadstead; above it stand harsh and powerful hills which descend in steps toward the green Conca d'Oro. In spite of the massive invasion of cement over recent decades, the 'Golden Shell' still offers as a whole a spectacular and evocative landscape. First the Sicanians, then the Cretans and Elymians, founded their colonies beside the bay. The Phoenicians were also strongly attracted to the place, and it became a permanent Phoenician colony in the eighth century B.C. Between the sixth and fourth centuries B.C. a new fortified city grew up around the original nucleus of the *Palaeopolis* and that of the more recently developed *Neapolis*. The Syracusans made several unsuccessful attempts to take the new city at the time of the wars against the Carthaginians. After a fruitless siege in 258 B.C., the stronghold of the Carthiginians in Sicily was forced to yield to the Romans in 254 B.C.; four years later the Romans resisted Hasdrubal's attempt to reconquer it. When Roman power declined, between the sixth and ninth centuries, Palermo fell into the hands of barbarian peoples (Vandals, Ostrogoths), who remained in power there in turn until the Byzantines took over in the first half of the sixth century, to be turned out themselves by the Arabs in 831. At the beginning of the eleventh century a combined military invasion by Normans and Pisans undermined the Arab occupation; the Arabs had given way to the Normans of Robert Guiscard and Roger by 1072. From that date till the last twenty years of the twelfth century the stage was held by the rise and fall of the Normans, who spread out from Palermo all over Sicily, promoting science, culture and the arts. When the Normans declined it was the turn of the Swabians; Frederick II was a great figure on the stage of history, a ruler who attracted the most talented and innovative men of the time, in spite of the combined opposition to him of nobles and papacy. When Frederick died (1250), the city declined inexorably until finally the capital was transferred to Naples (1266); the Angevins and Aragonese took their turns as rulers in Palermo. The brief interlude of the Vespers (1282) only consolidated the power of the Aragonese, which was a prelude to the long-lasting dominion of the Spanish in Palermo and on the island. Between the sixteenth and seventeenth centuries, the city changed its face again; new fortifications were built and the layout of the town changed substantially.

In the first half of the eighteenth century, the Savoys and the Austrians ruled until the advent of Charles III, who built his fortune on the foundation of arrogant abuses of power by clergy and nobility. In the second half of the eighteenth century the Spanish viceroy Caracciolo carried out a series of reforms of which the most striking was the suppression of the tribunal of the Holy Office. As a result of the French Revolution and widespread unrest in the island, the Bourbon rulers introduced a constitution in 1812; this, however, did not contain the revolutionary unrest and a fertile terrain was prepared for the victorious enterprise of Garibaldi (1860).

◄ An aerial photo of the Cathedral complex.

◄ The side toward the square.

The south porch, a Catalan Gothic work of the late fifteenth century.

Cathedral:- This majestic building is imposing for its dramatic outline and the way it rises at the end of the square of the same name (Piazza della Cattedrale), which was built over an ancient cemetery and is surrounded by a marble balustrade with sculptures in Baroque style on it. It was begun in 1184 by order of Archbishop Gualterio Offamilio (Walter of the Mill), on the site of a previous Muslim building, and is the product of a series of rebuildings, additions and modifications over many centuries. The four bell-towers were built in the fourteenth century; the south and north porches were built between the fifteenth and sixteenth centuries.

The *facade* dates from the fourteenth and fifteenth centuries and is framed by two bell-towers adorned with very fine carved motifs recalling Islamic decorations in the interweaving of plant and abstract elements. The splendid fifteenth-century portal is rich in decorative details in Gothic style. On the side toward the square is the **south porch**, a work of Catalan Gothic of great architectural importance (second half of the fifteenth century). The **apse** between the two towers is the most important portion remaining of the original Norman building. The **north porch** dates from the sixteenth century. The **interior** of the original building was very different from the present one, which is the result of considerable remodelling in the eighteenth century under the direction of F. Fuga. Divided into nave and aisles by a series of pillars, against which stand the Gagini statues of *Saints* (once part of a demolished apse), it is predominantly Neo-Classical in ap-

pearance. In the right aisle, in a bay to the left of the entrance from the square, are the *royal and imperial tombs*, to be exact those of Henry VI († 1197), Frederick II († 1250), the Empress Constance († 1198) and Roger († 1154). On the right side of the presbytery is the **Chapel of Santa Rosalia**, where a bronze railing protects the niche with the silver *urn* containing the mortal remains of the patron saint of the city.

On the right side of the apse is the entrance to the anteroom of the Sacristy, from which a magnificent fifteenth century portal leads into the **Treasury**, where rich vestments, altar cloths, holy vessels, monstrances, miniatures of the fourteenth to eighteenth centuries and other valuable objects can be seen. Next door, the **Sagrestia dei Canonici** (Sacristy of the Canons) has sixteenth century portals by V. Gagini. In the adjacent **Sagrestia Nuova** (New Sacristy) is a *Virgin* attributed to A. Gagini. In the left transept is the **Chapel of the Sacramento** which houses a precious seventeenth century lapislazuli ciborium, made by an artist from Bergamo and of very striking appearance. On the right is the eighteenth century *mausoleum of the Archbishop Sanseverino*, attributed to G. Pennino.

The **crypt** is later than the original building; it is entered on the left and has two transverse aisles divided by granite columns and a cross vault. It is worth noticing the seven little apses on the side opposite the entrance and the many monuments of archbishops of Palermo, including that of Gualtiero Offamilio, founder of the Cathedral.

Porta Nuova:- This spectacular construction stands at the beginning of Corso Catalafimi and is almost an appendix of the Palazzo dei Normanni. It was begun in the second half of the sixteenth century to commemorate the entry of Charles V to the city, almost fifty years earlier, through a fifteenth century gate that stood there at that time. The Porta Nuova as we see it today is a monumental construction which unites the characteristics of the triumphal arch with marked Renaissance elements. The interesting pyramidal crowning is decorated with majolica figures representing the *eagle*, the symbol of the senate of Palermo.

Palazzo dei Normanni:- This grandly monumental building, known also as the *Royal Palace*, probably arose on an ancient site in the ninth century, during the Arab period. From the eleventh century, the palace was the seat of the Norman and Swabian kings. Restored in the sixteenth century, it was from time to time the residence of viceroys and royal personages of various European houses. Since 1947 it has been the seat of the *Sicilian Regional Assembly*.

The Porta Nuova, built in the second half of the fifteenth century to celebrate Charles II's entry to the city.

The back of the Palazzo dei Normanni, built by Arabs and enlarged by the Normans in the twelfth century, with nineteenth century alterations.

Two views of the eighteenth century courtyard with its porticoes and loggias.

Next pages, Palatine Chapel: the central apse in the presbytery. On the right the ambo and the white marble candelabrum.

The Christ Blessing in the main apse, a Byzantine work of the twelfth century.

The **facade**, which is of strongly sixteenth century appearance, was several times remodelled and rebuilt from the seventeenth century on. On the right stands the **Torre Pisana** (Pisan Tower), also called *Torre di Santa Ninfa*, which is one of the most easily visible parts of the original Norman building. By way of an interesting seventeenth century courtyard, with porches and loggias, we come to an imposing staircase leading up to the first floor, where by far the most interesting portion of the whole complex is situated.

The **Palatine Chapel** is counted among the finest and most typical examples of Norman art in the Sicilian capital. It was begun in 1130 and consecrated in 1143. The outer walls of the chapel have been made partly invisible by later construction work; for example the seventeenth century facade has hidden the apse. The **interior** has a nave and aisles divided

12

14

The ambo in the nave supported by four pillars and the Romanesque candelabrum.

Two details of the very fine candelabrum for the Easter candle. It is the most ancient Romanesque sculpture in Sicily.

◄ *The* Christ Pantocrator *with archangels and angels in the dome.*

by ancient columns sustaining ogival arches; the same architectural traits find their highest expression in the raised sanctuary, the triple apse and the dome. The ornamentation of the chapel is marked by the extraordinary quality and beauty of its mosaics, and the very fine wooden *ceiling* (twelfth century), the work of Fatimite craftsmen. The most important of the mosaic decorations, carried out by Byzantine artists in the twelfth century, include the *Christ the Pantocrator with Archangels and Angels* (in the dome) and the *episodes from the life of Christ* in the apse and on the walls of the sanctuary. On the left side of the apse is the *'Madonna Hodigitria'*, while the walls of the nave represent Bible stories. In the aisles, the subjects of the mosaics are *episodes from the lives of St. Peter and St. Paul*. We observe the beautiful floors, also mosaic, the ambo (twelfth century), and the

Stories from the lives of Saints Peter and Paul *adorn the aisles of the Chapel.*

The insides of the arches are decorated with figures of saints.

Details of the walls of the nave with scenes from the Bible ►
on two fasciae.

Easter candlestick, which possess fine architectural and sculptural qualities. A small staircase below the ambo leads to the **Crypt**, where the remains of William I once lay; they were later removed to the Cathedral of Monreale. The *Crucifix* on the wall is from the sixteenth century. In the **Sacristy** rooms we can see a valuable *Treasury* with vestments and altar cloths, silver vessels, finally worked caskets in Arab and Byzantine style and parchments.

There are rooms of considerable interest on the second floor of the Palazzo dei Normanni also; we will mention the so-called **Salone d'Ercole**, the walls and ceiling of which are decorated with frescoes representing the legends of the mythical Hercules who gave his name to the room, which is now the seat of the deliberations of the Sicilian Regional Assembly. The room was built in the second half of the six-

teenth century, and Giuseppe Velasquez painted the frescoes on the walls and ceiling in the eighteenth century. Around the sixteenth century **Cortile della Fontana** (Courtyard of the Fountain) lie the apartments of the 'piano nobile', which have eighteenth and nineteenth century furnishings and decorations. We can visit also the **Room of the Viceroys**, where the portraits of the viceroys are exhibited. Across an atrium dominated by a turreted structure which is part of the Palace, we reach the splendid **Sala di Re Ruggero** (Room of King Roger), magnificently decorated with rich mosaics in Arab style representing hunting scenes.

The **Torre Pisana**, in which an **Astronomical Observatory** is situated, dominates another room which is rather bare in appearance, although a few vestiges still suggest the rich marble and mosaic decorations that once adorned the walls. Restoration work carried out during the seventies of this century permits us to appreciate, from the first floor, the chronology of the various constructions and additions that this part of the building has undergone over the centuries. Among other rooms, we should note the **Sala degli Armigeri** and the **Sala del Tesoro**. (Squires' Room and Treasury).

◀ *In front of the main apse is the royal throne. It was probably made at the Aragonese period.*

The "Room of King Roger" in the Palazzo dei Normanni. The walls are lined with marble; lunettes, tympana and vaults are covered in magnificent twelfth century mosaics.

◄ *"Room of King Roger": one of the lunettes with a pattern of flowers and peacocks.*

◄ *"Room of King Roger": the golden decoration of the vault.*

Next pages, the ceiling painted to imitate mosaic with floral patterns in the "Room of the Four Winds".

21

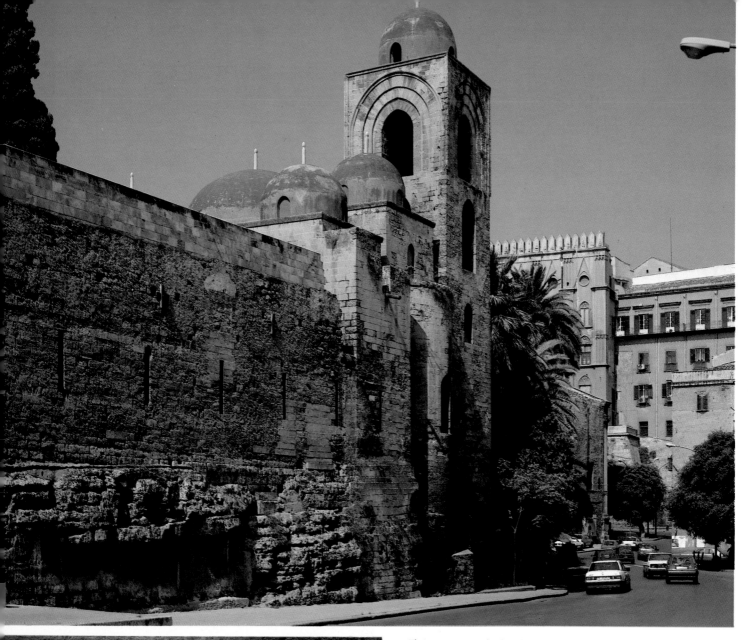

The very unusual Church of San Giovanni degli Eremiti was built for Roger II in 1132 by Arab craftsmen; this is the inside of one of its characteristic domes.

Church of San Giovanni degli Eremiti:- This church of the Norman period was built by order of Roger in the first half of the twelfth century, on the site of a previous Gregorian monastery. Considerably remodelled in the second half of last century, it is a typical example of Muslim architecture and was built by Arab craftsmen who were active at that time in Palermo. The bell tower is a simple, austere structure with lancet windows in its sides; it is crowned by a small red dome which combines with the other domes in the complex to give the whole building a strongly Oriental appearance.

The *interior* is extremely simple and without ornamentation. Two great ogival arches span the single nave, while the transept is divided into three apses of semicircular form. On the right side of the transept is the entrance to some rooms outside the church on the right, which can be identified as the remains of an ancient building of the tenth or eleventh century. It is highly doubtful that they were once part of a mosque. The fine **Cloister** is also Norman (thirteenth century) and is part of an ancient Benedictine monastery. The lovely, lush garden, full of greenery, is surrounded by rows of little ogival arches supported by elegant twin columns.

One of the Oriental-looking red domes and the evocative thirteenth century cloister of San Giovanni degli Eremiti.

Two views of Piazza Pretoria with the monumental fountain adorned with statues by sixteenth century Florentine artists.

Palazzo Senatorio:- The present seat of city government overlooks the *Piazza Pretoria*, which is enhanced by the fountain of the same name. The building arose in the second half of the fifteenth century, probably on the site of a previous Aragonese palace. Several times altered (sixteenth, seventeenth and nineteenth centuries), it has a sumptuous facade; works that stand out are the seventeenth century *statue of St. Rosalia* attributed to Carlo d'Aprile, and the marble *eagle* over the door, the work of Salvatore Valenti, while some inscriptions on plaques commemorate important events in the city's history.

Important art works in the interior include Sozzo's frescoes (sixteenth century) in the **atrium**, the fine Baroque *portal* by Amato (seventeenth century), and a funerary sculpture in marble, probably of the Roman period. We should note, finally, the allegorical sculpture representing the *Genius of Palermo* (first landing on the stairs), and the **Sala delle Lapidi, Sala Gialla** and **Sala di Garibaldi** (Plaque Room, Yellow Room and Garibaldi Room). From the balcony of this room, the famous condottiere of the Risorgimento harangued the crowds in Palermo on the 30th of May, 1860.

Fontana Pretoria:- Originally designed for the Florentine residence of Don Pietro di Toledo, this fountain was then bought by the Senate of Palermo, which placed it in front of its own building. A spectacular and superb work of the sixteenth century, it was made by the Florentine artists Francesco Cammil-

The exterior of the Church of Santa Maria dell'Ammiraglio, known as "La Martorana".

One of the mosaics in the arches depicting the Death of the Virgin.

liani and Michelangelo Naccerino, who created masterful allegorical, mythological and monstrous sculptures to adorn it. The railing surrounding it is a nineteenth century addition by G.B.F. Basile.

Church of Santa Maria dell'Ammiraglio:- Known also as *La Martorana*, this church was founded in the first half of the twelfth century by Roger's admiral, George of Antioch. The present appearance of the building is eclectic, combining features of the elevated Norman architectural style and Baroque elements added later. The *facade*, which is obviously Baroque in origin, is from the second half of the sixteenth century. The very fine *Bell tower* has four storeys, lightened by the play of the lancet windows, the slim pillars and the colourful inlays.

The *interior*, also substantially altered by Baroque remodelling, is divided into a nave and two aisles and is particularly memorable for its mosaics. On the right wall, beyond an ancient door, is the mosaic of *Christ crowning Roger II*; on the left wall are a *Madonna of the Rosary* attributed to Zoppo di Gangi and a mosaic representing *George of Antioch at the feet of the Virgin*. The dome, the tambour, the vault and the two small apses are all decorated with beautiful mosaics on religious subjects. In the upper choir (eighteenth century) are many paintings of that date by G. Borremans, who also frescoed the middle portion of the building.

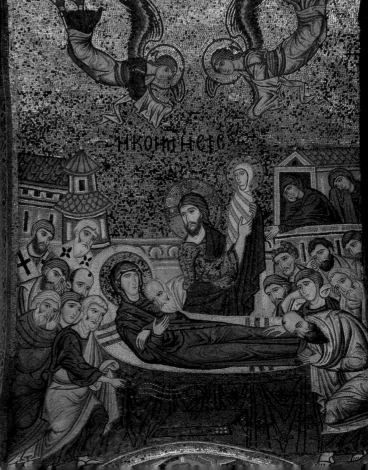

The vault with Christ Blessing and
the Four Archangels; and the Nativity
in the arch.

The Normán mosaic in the church of ►
"La Martorana" showing Roger II
crowned by Jesus.

The entrance to the Regional Gallery of Sicily is in the Late Gothic-Renaissance courtyard of Palazzo Abatellis.

The famous bust of Eleanor of Aragon, the work of Francesco Laurana (fifteenth century).

Regional Gallery of Sicily:- The Regional Gallery of Sicily is housed in the fifteenth century Palazzo Abatelis, built in 1490-1495 by Matteo Carnelivari, a fine example of the blending of the Late Gothic and Renaissance architectural styles. This Gallery possesses the most important collection on the island of sculpture and painting, especially of the fourteenth to sixteenth centuries. The sculpture is exhibited on the ground floor, and the painting gallery is on the first floor.

Room I: sixteenth century paintings and wooden sculptures.

Room II: This is the chapel of the palace; it contains some fourteenth and fifteenth century sculptures (particularly interesting is the *sarcophagus of Cecilia Aprile*, attributed to Francesco Laurana) and the impressive fresco of the *Triumph of Death*, of uncertain attribution, perhaps by a collaborator of Pisanello, dating from the mid-fifteenth century.

Room III: various works, outstanding among which is a magnificent Malaga vase with a metallic sheen ("loza dorada") and a Spanish-Arab jar, both from the thirteenth-fourteenth centuries.

Room IV: here we find the very famous *bust of Eleanor of Aragon*, a masterpiece by Francesco Laurana dating from about 1471; it is accompanied by a fine *Portrait of a Gentlewoman*, attributed to Laurana, and other fifteenth century sculptures of the school of the Gaginis.

Room V: a *Madonna and Child* and a *Portrait of a Girl*, marble statues by Antonello Gagini.

Room VI: more works by the Gaginis and by Lombard masters of the end of the fifteenth century.

Room VII and **Room VIII**: paintings of various origins, especially Venetian, Tuscan and Sicilian of the fourteenth and fifteenth centuries.

Room IX: a vast hall in which a series of works by Tommaso de Vigilia, an important late fifteenth century painter from Palermo, stand out.

Room X: This is the room devoted to the *Virgin of the Annunciation*, the great masterpiece of Antonello da Messina, painted around 1473, in which space and light are fused around the figure and face of the Virgin.

Room XI and **XII**: various works by Sicilian masters of the end of the fifteenth century and the beginning of the sixteenth, among which those of Riccardo Quartararo of Sciacca are worth pointing out.

Room XIII: dedicated to Flemish painting; the very famous *Malvagna Triptych* by Jan Gossaert holds the attention.

Rooms XIV, XV and **XVI**: other works by Flemish artists and sixteenth and seventeenth century Italian masters (worth mentioning are Vincenzo da Pavia, Jacopo Palma il Giovane, Mattia Preti).

There is a plan to enlarge the Gallery to include seventeenth and eighteenth century painting, sections for decorative arts, etc.

The masterpiece among the Gallery's paintings, the Virgin of the Annunciation *by Antonello da Messina.*

In the Palace chapel is the mid-fifteenth century fresco of The Triumph of Death.

The head of a warrior from the excavations at Himera.

Metope from Selinunte with Perseus, helped by Athena, killing the Medusa.

The so-called Ephebus of Selinunte, a fine little bronze of 460 B.C.

Regional Archaeological Museum:- The museum is housed in the restored *Convent of the Filippini dell'Olivella* and offers us a very interesting collection of Sicilian antiquities in general and of sculptures from Selinunte in particular.

In the ***Greek Epigraph Room*** are interesting inscriptions from Selinunte.

The adjacent ***Room of the Bicephalous Selinunte Steles*** houses two-headed steles from Selinunte.

In the ***Marconi Room*** are architectural fragments and bronze heads found at the Temple of the Victory of Himera (fifth century B.C.). In the ***Gabrici Room*** we find architectural fragments from Selinunte; this leads into the ***Selinunte Room***, which houses the sculptures from the temples of Selinunte.

First floor: We ascend to the ***North Gallery***, where finds from Solunto and the necropolises of Bagheria, Himera and Termini Imerese are displayed.

In the ***Terracotta Room*** we find antiquities of various origins. In the ***Gallery of Selinunte Terracotta*** are many terracotta objects (ex votos) from the Selinunte area.

The ***Sculpture Rooms*** house objects of Greek and Roman origin.

Second floor: Admirable examples of the prehistoric art of Sicily, from the Palaeolithic to the Bronze Age, are exhibited in the different rooms.

The ***Greek ceramic collections*** include Attic vases with the typical red and black figures, as well as Italiot, proto-

Corinthian, Corinthian, Ionian and Laconian works.

In the **Mosaic Room** we find frescoes from Selinunte similar to those of Pompeii and mosaic decorations found at Palermo.

In the **Himera Room** are finds from the various temples of Himera.

Monastery and crypt of the Capuchins:- The monastery of the Capuchins (built in 1621) is known above all for its catacombs, although the church, which has been considerably altered in modern times, preserves various fine church ornaments, for example wooden altars of the eighteenth and nineteenth centuries and a reliquiary, also wooden, of the eighteenth century, which are worth noting. In the catacombs are piled the corpses, some of them partially mummified, some embalmed, of about eight thousand clerics and members of the rich bourgeoisie of Palermo, including women and children, who from the seventeenth century up to 1881, when the macabre custom was made illegal, were buried in the crypt of this monastery. Impressionable people are advised not to visit these long rows of dead bodies.

Two macabre views of the approximately eight thousand mummified corpses in the crypt of the Capuchin Monastery.

The Chinese Pavilion in the park of La Favorita, built by Ferdinand II of Bourbon.

Palazzina Cinese:- In the upper part of the huge park, **Parco della Favorita** (which possesses green space for public use and sports installations), on the slopes of Monte Pellegrino, rises this distinctive small palace built by the architect V. Marvuglia between the end of the eighteenth century and the beginning of the nineteenth century. He gave it the combination, typical at that time, of Neo-Classical regularity with a taste for everything exotic and connected with the East. In the rooms, we note the decorations in different styles, furniture of the time and a collection of Chinese and English silks and prints. The frescoes which enhance some of the rooms were painted by V. Riolo, G. Patania and G. Velasquez.

Pitré Ethnographic Museum:- This interesting collection was founded by Pitré in 1909 and is housed in a building to the right of the Palazzina Cinese, in the Parco della Favorita.

In **Room I** are furnishings and models of rustic houses.

In **Room II** we can see yarns and weavings with the tools used in making them.

In **Room III** we find interesting costumes of the island.

In **Room IV** are festival costumes, embroidery and ornaments.

In **Room V** is a collection of Christmas costumes.

In **Room VI** hunting implements are displayed.

Room VII focuses on fishing; we find implements, boats and interesting miniatures.

Room VIII accomodates models of ploughs and agricultural implements.

In **Room IX** the implements used in sheep-farming are exhibited.

Rooms X-XI display the tools for itinerant arts, trades and commerce.

In **Rooms XII-XV** we find objects connected with magic and religion, talismans against spells and the evil eye, ex votos, masks.

Rooms XVI-XVII are laid out to represent a rustic kitchen.

In **Room XVIII** we can see Christmas cribs; there is a particularly interesting eighteenth century one from Trapani.

Room XIX displays costumes, statues and other objects connected with the Easter processions.

In **Room XX** the costumes of the confraternities and some wooden statues are on show.

In **Room XXI** we find articles connected with the chariots of the religious processions; there is a wooden model of the car of Santa Rosalia.

In **Room XXII** is a puppet theatre.

Room XXIII displays the decorations of the Sicilian cart and an example of one.

Rooms XXIV-XXVII are decorated as a bourgeois apartment of the seventeenth century.

In **Rooms XXVIII-XXXII** are various objects in terracotta.

Room XXXIII exhibits intaglios and other handicrafts.

In **Room XXXIV** musical instruments are displayed.

On the **first floor** in **Rooms XXXV-XL** is a well stocked library on subjects of ethnography and Italian and foreign folklore.

In **Room XXXIX** we can see documents with Pitré's signature and many letters.

MONDELLO

A pleasant bathing and residential centre, Mondello enjoys a picturesque situation facing the bay between Punta Valdesi and the fishing centre. The town itself is practically part of the capital; long, straight roads join it to Palermo, crossing the beautiful Parco della Favorita or following the coast road below Monte Pellegrino which goes by **Vergine Maria** (on the right, on the slope of the mountain, is the monumental cemetery called *Cimitero dei Rotoli*) and **Arenella**. In the oldest part of the town, where we can see the colourful boats of the fishermen, are two **watch-towers** built in the fifteenth century as part of the coastal defense works. Projecting into the sea in the centre of the bay is the distinctive outline of the *bathing establishment*, built in 1912. To the east of **Valdesi**, on the coast road, we find in the slopes of Mount Pellegrino the **Grotte dell'Addaura** (Addaura Caves), which have provided significant proof of the presence of human beings in the area since prehistoric times; the finds from the caves can be seen in the Archaeological Museum in the capital.

The picturesque bay (with Mount Pellegrino in the background) and the port of the town.

The facade of the Norman Cathedral, second half of the twelfth century.

The splendid bronze door and the aisled nave of the Cathedral. ▶

The central apse with the mosaic of Christ Pantocrator. ▶

Next pages, two close-up views of the majestic Christ Pantocrator which entirely covers the vault of the central apse.

MONREALE

This picturesque town immediately inland from Palermo spreads over the lower slopes of the hills that rise into the ring of calcareous mountains surrounding the Conca d'Oro. Although the Conca d'Oro itself has become in recent decades nothing more than a configuration of the terrain, because of the inexorable advance of concrete paving and buildings which have reduced to a few gardens and isolated green patches the huge spread of citrus farms that gave it its name, Monreale is still exceptional for its pleasant natural setting, the beauty of its panorama and the splendour of its art treasures. It grew up in Norman times around a Benedictine monastery and became the favourite abode of the Norman kings, who often went hunting there. It is known today for its Cathedral and Cloister, one of the main attractions for visitors to the island, its beautiful surroundings and the distinctive character of its buildings, basically medieval with the addition of houses and other buildings of the Baroque period. The **Duomo** (Cathedral), counted among the purest manifestations of Norman art in Sicily, was built under the auspices of William II in the second half of the twelfth century. Its most distinctive features are the extremely beautiful mosaics which cover the inside walls, creating a fairy-tale atmosphere,

and its graceful architectural forms, which show the Fatimite and Muslim influence common at the time. The upper part of the **facade** is an example of an recurrent Arabic ornamental motif, the interlaced arches, while the porch on the lower part, added in the second half of the eighteenth century, creates a link between two powerful turreted structures. These structures, although the left one remained unfinished, complete the picture of the front of the church, defining it spatially and giving a sense of balance to the whole, in spite of the dubiously valid eighteenth century addition. The very beautiful portal is enhanced by a splendid bronze door, the work of Bonanno Pisano, of the second half of the twelfth century. A Gagini portico runs down the left side of the building, where we find the entrance to the church. The door is by Barisano da Trani (second half of the twelfth century). The exterior of the apse is finely decorated with lava stone inlays and interlaced arches.

The **interior** of the basilica is majestic and solemn. The Latin cross of its plan is divided into three lengthwise by ancient columns with marvellously carved capitals which support ogival arches. The upper part of the sanctuary is outstanding for its colours and its decorative and architectural qualities; from the ceiling of the main apse the severe gaze of *Christ the Pantocrator* reaches into every hidden corner of the building, and gives the impression by a curious optical illusion of

A view of the nave toward the entrance.

Mosaics in the nave with stories from the Old Testament. ▶

looking into the visitor's eyes wherever he is standing. The impressive expanse of mosaics on a gold ground is the fruit of the patient work of Byzantine and Arab craftsmen during the twelfth and thirteenth centuries. Besides the already mentioned figure of Christ the Pantocrator, below which is the *Virgin Enthroned with Saints, Apostles and Angels*, we find, in the nave, Biblical episodes from the Old and New Testament and stories of the Norman kings: above the royal throne is the *Crowning of William II*, and above the archbishop's throne *William II Offering the Church to the Virgin*. The wooden trusses of the ceiling are from the first half of last century and replace the original ones, ruined by fire. The marble floor, with mosaic decorations, dates in part from the sixteenth century. From the right aisle we enter the **Chapel of San Castrense** (sixteenth century), adorned by a ciborium of the same date and a seventeenth century painting by P.A. Novelli of the saint of the same name. From the end of the right transept we enter the **Chapel of the Benedictines**, which contains admirable marble bas-reliefs by Giovanni Marino

and Ignazio Marabitti (*Sarcophagus of F. Testa, Sarcophagus of I. Bonanno, Apotheosis of San Benedetto*). In the right aisle of the transept are the *tombs of William I and William II*, while the altar in the right apse has Baroque traits. In the centre of the apse we find the high altar, designed by Valadier (second half of the eighteenth century). The altar in the left apse is Baroque and has a wooden *Crucifix* above it; there is also a marble reliquiary from the workshop of Gagini, representing the *Pietà*, the *Annunciation and Sts. Peter and Paul*. There follow the altar of *Louis IX* and the sarcophagi of *Margaret, Roger* and *Henry of Navarre*. From the **Chapel of the Crucifix**, on the left side of the apse, we enter the **Treasury**, where precious objects of the Norman and Baroque periods are displayed. At the beginning of the right aisle we find the entrance to the stairs to the **terraces** and the top of the Cathedral, from which we enjoy splendid views of the Cloisters, Monreale and the Conca d'Oro.

The attached **Benedictine Abbey** was built at the same time as the Cathedral and underwent various additions up to at

◄ *Two views of the beautiful Benedictine cloister adjacent to the cathedral of Monreale, built at the end of the twelfth century. Particularly fine is the workmanship of the 228 twin columns, the capitals and the graceful fountain.*

The fountain in the middle of a small enclosure in the cloister, and details of capitals of the 48 little columns where religious and profane themes alternate and blend with rare charm.

43

The sumptuous seventeenth century Chapel of the Crucifix in the Cathedral.

The thirteenth century apse of the Cathedral. ▶

least the end of the fourteenth century. The most interesting part of it is the splendid Cloister, which we enter on the right of the Cathedral (from the front). The elegant rows of twin columns support ogival arches of exquisite Arab workmanship; the whole is enhanced by mosaics and lively capitals carved by Byzantine and Islamic artists. At the end of the cloister, inside a court, is a very fine fountain with Moorish and Hispanic characteristics.

The **Chiesa del Monte** is in Baroque taste; the interior of the church is enlivened by stucco decorations by P. Serpotta.

The **Collegiata**, originally built in the seventeenth century, was remodelled later; good paintings and wooden sculptures are preserved there.

The **Church of San Castrense** is also Baroque and possesses an interesting painting by Novelli and stucco ornaments from the Serpotta workshop.

The small **Church of San Antonio** has a graceful eighteenth century Baroque facade. An admirable view can be enjoyed from the public gardens of the **Belvedere**.

The **Abbey of San Martino delle Scale**, a village which has become a holiday resort on the spurs of the hills above Monreale and the plain of Palermo, dates from the second half of the eighteenth century and was built by Venanzio Marvuglia who enlarged a previously existing Benedictine building erected, according to some sources, by Gregory the Great in the sixth century. In the sixteenth century church we find admirable canvases by Zoppo di Gangi, Filippo Paladino and Pietro Novelli.

The remains of the ancient city of Solunto, a colony of Magna Grecia.

The Villa Palagonia at Bagheria, with its strange statues of ▶
dwarfs and monasters.

SOLUNTO

Solunto is a zone of great archaeological interest on the ter-
rassed slopes of Mount Catalfano, a site of great beauty for
its landscapes and views.

The first settlements here were very probably Phoenician.
Later a Punic stronghold together with nearby Palermo and
Motye, it was first conquered by the Syracusans (fourth century B.C.) and then by the Romans (third century B.C.). The
place went into a rapid decline and was completely abandoned in the second century B.C. Recent archaeological
studies allow us to dismiss the hypothesis that the most ancient nucleus was in fact at the nearby locality called Pizza
Cannita. The excavations have brought to light the remains
of an ancient settlement of urban character, similar to those
of other archaeological zones in the island. They can be de-
fined as late Classical in type, with Hellenistic and Roman
additions.

In the **Antiquarium** we can see the finds from the archaeological explorations. The **Gymnasium** is in part the result of
reconstruction in the second half of last century; its name derives from an inscription found there. Among the many houses
the **Casa di Leda** is outstanding. It was brought to light in the
early sixties of this century, and its name derives from the
subjects of some paintings from the first century A.D.found
in an inside room. It is also worth nothing the vestiges of the
small **Theatre**, once capable of seating 1200 people, and the
nearby **Bouleuterion**, where the meetings of the senate were
held. It is believed that in the highest part of the archaeological area there was an **Acropolis** and together with it the oldest part of the settlement.

BAGHERIA

This is a densely populated agro-industrial centre on the
southern slopes of Mount Catalfano, which here extend to the
sea, forming the eastern boundary of the Gulf of Palermo.
The town, which is situated in an area of large citrus groves,
became important in the seventeenth century, when the nobility of Palermo chose to reside there because of the favourable climate. Thus in a brief time many villas and residences
were built and the nobles escaped there from the summer
heat. The town grew up in the shadow of the house of Branciforti of Butera, and developed considerably between the
end of the seventeenth and beginning of the eighteenth centuries, when a number of opulent houses were built.

The **Villa Gravina di Palagonia** is from the first half of the
eighteenth century and is marked by an elliptical plan. The
facade has classical features, while some of the sculptural
decorations are fantastic or monstrous.

The **Villa Gravina di Valguarnera**, which was built in the early eighteenth century, recalls in the rich articulation of its facade and its architectural layout in general the architecture
of the Renaissance. The carvings which adorn the facade are
the work of Marabitti.

The **Villa Bonanni di Cattolica** is also from the first half of
the eighteenth century; its rooms have been used to house
a Gallery of Modern and Contemporary Art with works by
Guttuso, who was born in this town, and other artists of our
times.

The **Villa Branciforti di Butera**, built in the second half of
the seventeenth century, stands out among the other noble
houses.

CEFALÙ

This charming and graceful little town faces the Tyrrhenian sea from a promontory overhung by a huge, rough outcrop of the mountains. Because of its favourable climate and outstanding natural and artistic features, it is counted among the touristic jewels of the Palermo province. It carries on a flourishing tourist trade, while its other economic activities are fishing and farming. The origins of the place are very ancient, dating perhaps from prehistoric times; there are references around the fourth century B.C. to a *Cephaloedion* allied to the Carthaginians in the war against Syracuse. The placename is obviously connected with the peculiar shape of the rock that gives the town its character. Subjected by the Syracusans, it went through various stages before becoming a satellite of Rome (third century B.C.). In the second half of the ninth century A.D. it gravitated to the Arab emirate of the capital. Taken over by the Normans (eleventh century), the town grew considerably and had many large buildings added to it; it later became a feud of the powerful houses of Chiaramonte and Ventimiglia. In the second half of last century Cefalù took an active if not very successful part in the revolt against the Bourbons.

The facade and interior of the Cathedral of Cefalù, a Norman work begun in the twelfth century.

The imposing structure of the Cathedral, and the apse with the Byzantine mosaic of Christ Pantocrator.

The magnificent **Cathedral** has the usual structural and architectural characteristics of Norman religious buildings, and is in many ways similar to the Cathedral of Monreale. Begun in the first half of the twelfth century, in the time of Roger II, it took a very long time to build and remained in the end partially unfinished. A flight of steps leads to the parvis which is fenced and adorned with statues. The superb *facade* (thirteenth century) is framed between two powerful towers lightened by rows of lancet windows. Its upper part is adorned with small blind arches and interlaced arches of obviously Muslim descent. The lower portico with its ogival arches is from the second half of the fifteenth century and is attributed to Ambrogio da Como. Other outstanding architectural features of the building include the right side, the powerful transept and the triple apse.

The monumental *interior* has the characteristics of a basilica; the nave is divided from the aisles by powerful columns with artistic capitals of Roman and Corinthian type. These support elegant ogival arches which reveal Arab influence. In the left aisle is a sixteenth century *Virgin* by Antonello Gagini, while in the right aisle the *baptismal font* (1100) is of particular interest. The entrance to the transept is through a powerful

ogival arcade with colossal columns. The presbytery is raised and glows with the luminous mosaics in Byzantine style that adorn it. The floor is also mosaic; on it stand the royal throne and the bishop's throne, also enhanced by mosaic inlays. The subjects of the priceless gold-ground mosaics are: in the apse, *Christ the Pantocrator* in the blessing posture surrounded by the *Virgin, Apostles and Archangels*, and on the walls of the tribune, series of *Patriarchs, Prophets and Saints*.

The beautiful adjacent **Cloister** uses very charming architectural elements, especially the rows of small twin columns sustaining graceful ogival arches. We observe particularly the carvings on the capitals, which represent fantastic subjects, mythological figures and fights betwen animals.

The **Osterio Magno** is what is left of a graceful palace of the Norman period, believed to be the residence of Roger (twelfth century) although some sources suggest that it was constructed later (fourteenth century). Of particular interest are the fine lancet windows of the old building.

The **Mandralisca Museum** contains valuable paintings of the fifteenth to eighteenth centuries; outstanding in the collection is an admirable work attributed to Antonello da Messina, the *Portrait of an Unknown Man*. There are also fragments of mosaic paving from Roman times, icons in Byzantine style and a large number of finds of archaeological interest from around the town and from Lipari. In particular we should take note of a Greek mosaic of the second to first century B.C, and the Lipari bowl with a picture of a *Seller of Tunny Fish*, an important example of Siceliot pottery of the fourth century B.C. Finally there are Sicilian coins, prehistoric finds, lanterns and other objects of the Greek and Roman ages, vases, clay objects, sulptures, bas-reliefs and Siceliot pottery.

Substantial vestiges remain of the polygonal **walls** of the ancient settlement, dating from the fourth century B.C.

On the rock above the town we can see the remains of a megalithic construction of the fourth to third century B.C., known as the **Temple of Diana**.

The whole coast around Cefalù is dotted with first rank hotels, residences and organized tourist villages.

On the mountain slopes behind the town and reachable by a winding road is the **Sanctuary of Gibilmanna** (seventeenth century), which has a fine altar and a *Virgin* by the Gaginis. The name of the place is of Arab derivation and refers to the presence there of quantities of ash 'manna'.

◄ *Two panoramic views of Cefalù and its ancient town.*

The famous Greek vase with the scene of the vendor of tuna fish (fourth century B.C.), and an Attic crater (480-470 B.C.), in the Mandralisca Museum at Cefalù.

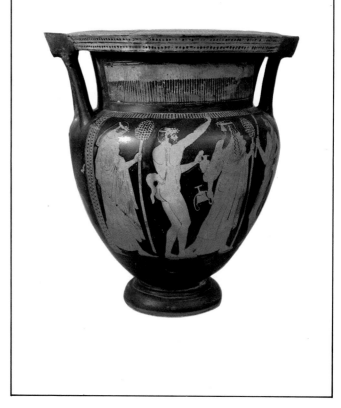

The little port and the "Faraglioni" of the island of Ustica.

ISLAND OF USTICA

This island rises from the waters of the Tyrrhenian about 36 miles to the north-west of Palermo and has a wild and fascinating appearance because of the contrast between the intense colours of the sea and the rough volcanic rock formations of its coast (it is geologically similar to Lipari).

The earliest inhabitants there were the Phoenicians; later the Greeks called it *Osteodes*, or the 'ossuary', in memory of the six thousand deported Carthaginians who are traditionally believed to have died of inanition on the island. The Romans gave it the name of *Ustum*, a reference to the blackish, burnt appearance of its volcanic rocks. There was once a Benedictine monastery on the island, around which the first settlement formed; the settlement was several times razed by Saracen pirates. In the second half of the eighteenth century, Ustica was fortified by the Bourbons, which thus allowed organized colonies of settlers from Palermo, Trapani and the Aeolian islands to form.

The town called Ustica is on the north-east coast and slopes picturesquely down the folds of the **Falconara**, a tufa relief where the remains of an ancient **Necropolis** with underground tombs have been found. An interesting **Museum of Submarine Archaeology** has been set up in the **Torre di Santa Maria**.

A remote prehistoric settlement dating from the Bronze Age (fourteenth to thirteenth century B.C.) has been identified in the place called **Faraglioni**.

Panorama of the port and sea-front at Trapani.

TRAPANI

Historical note:- The city projects like a wedge into the sea, opposite the Egadi (Aegatian) archipelago and between the slopes of Eryx and the narrow isthmus which overlooks the Lilybaean coast with its extensive salt-flats. An ancient seat of Sicanians and Elymians, it was called *Drepanon* by the Greeks, who were impressed by its sickle form. In the first half of the third century B.C. the city, by then in Punic hands, saw its population considerably increased by the massive migration of people from Eryx ordered by Hamilcar. Long disputed during the Punic wars, it was finally won by the Romans at the naval Battle of the Aegatian Islands (second half of the third century B.C.).

When Roman power declined, various other peoples passed through Trapani, and in the process the city developed a strong business sense. Already important under the Arabs and the Normans, it flourished particularly under the house of Aragon. In the sixteenth century the city was much favoured by Charles V, who also contributed to reinforcing its defense works. In following centuries Trapani further developed its sea trade, its fishing activities and the mining activities connected with the natural abundance of salt in its territory. During the Risorgimento it participated actively in the popular uprisings against the Bourbons. It unfortunately suffered con-

siderable damage during the campaigns of the Second World War, and has today a basically modern appearance, especially on the low coastal land where the urban plan is based on a wide grid. In the peninsular portion, the lay of the land imposes a closer structure, with narrow streets and characteristic alleys.

An important commercial, fishing and tourist port (it is the starting point for trips to the Egadi Islands opposite), it pursues a certain amount of industrial activity, connected with the processing of rural products, salt mining (although this is declining) and fishing. Craft activities include principally coral and mother-of-pearl work (in spite of decreases in recent years), pottery, whistles and marble work. The places where the people of Trapani meet and take their evening walk are concentrated around Via Torrearsa, Corso Vittorio Emmanuele and the panoramic Viale Regina Elena. The Piazza del Mercato del Pesce offers daily the spectacle of fish being sold in a colourful and picturesque setting. In the Rione Palma, every Thursday, the characteristic market of the itinerant vendors is held. In the field of foklore we have the well known *Processione dei Misteri*, which takes place on Good Friday and Easter Saturday. A feature of the procession are the groups of wooden sculptures.

Some views of the coast of Trapani, where salt is still being mined.

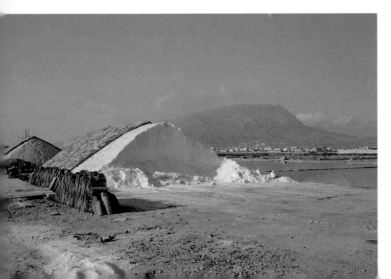

Sanctuary of the Annunziata:- The most important building in the town rises opposite the gardens of Villa Pepoli, almost at the eastern boundary of the built-up area. It was built in the first half of the fourteenth century, but the church as it appears today is the result of almost total remodelling in the second half of the eighteenth century.

The *facade*, adorned with a rose-window and a Gothic portal, is all that is left of the original building; it is flanked by a bell tower of pure Baroque characteristics with a pyramidal crowning. On the left side of the building we find the graceful apse of the Sailors' Chapel.

The *interior*, which has a single nave, has Baroque and Rococo ornamental features. The **Chapel of the Madonna**, which is behind the high altar, is the most artistically significant part of the complex. A sixteenth century bronze railing marks off the marble arch of the same period, richly decorated by the Gaginis. The votive chapel, splendidly enhanced by polychrome marble decorations and roofed by a vault of Arab type, preserves the venerated sculpted image of the *Madonna of Trapani*. This very beautiful sculpture of the *Virgin and Child* is believed to be a fourteenth century work by Nino Pisano or his followers. In an adjacent chapel, decorated with multicoloured marble inlays, is the silver image of *St. Alberto*, patron saint of the city. On the left side of the presbytery is the **Sailors' Chapel** (sixteenth century), which has a magnificently ornamented apse. On the right side is the Late Gothic **Fishermen's Chapel** (fifteenth century, frescoed in the following century).

The "Castello del Balio" or Pepoli Castle, built over the Temple of Venus of Eryx, *from which a splendid panorama may be admired.*

ERICE 3/15/2000

The classical Eryx, this little town is of great interest to tourists and rises at the top of the mountain of the same name, in a setting with a spectacular landscape and views. It is known that there were already Elymian settlements in the area in the fifth century B.C.; because of its special strategic importance it was the object of recurrent conflicts from ancient times, and in particular of the wars between Greeks and Carthaginians. It was taken by the latter, together with its port of *Drepanon*. Destroyed by the Carthaginians in the first half of the third century B.C., when its inhabitants were transferred to Trapani, it was at the centre of constant fighting with the Romans, who held it after 241 B.C. In Roman times the place was much visited because the celebrated Sanctuary of the Venus of Eryx was there. In medieval times it belonged first to the Arabs and then the Normans, and was called *Monte San Giuliano*.

The fame of the place is connected also with the *Centro Internazionale di Cultura Scientifica 'Ettore Majorana'* (Ettore Majorana International Centre for Scientific Culture), founded there in the sixties. Speaking of folklore, the best known event is the *Processione dei Misteri*, held on Good Friday. Typical craft products are the pottery, the *frazzate* (carpets) and the bags.

The **Chiesa Matrice** is a church of fourteenth century origin; beside it is a powerful battlemented tower pierced by lancet windows. In front of the church, which has a fine rose-window in the middle of the facade, is an ogival-arched porch with Gothic features, added in the fifteenth century, under which we come to the very fine Gothic portal. The interior, which has an aisled nave, is the product of rebuilding in Neo-Gothic style during last century. In the right aisle, on the third altar, is a *Virgin* believed to be the work of Laurana (fifteenth century). In the left aisle we find fifteenth and sixteenth century chapels. The sixteenth century marble altar-piece in the presbytery is by G. Mancino.

The **Church of San Giovanni Battista** is a building of the Norman Gothic period, and preserves the original door from that time (thirteenth century). Largely remodelled in the seventeenth century, it possesses important sculptures, the most interesting of which are a *St. John the Evangelist* by Antonello Gagini and a *Baptist* by Antonio Gagini.

The **city walls** date from various periods. There is little left of the megalithic walls of the sixth century B.C.; they were mostly rebuilt in the Roman and Norman periods.

Inside the so-called "Castello del Balio", (Castle of Venus), a Norman construction of the twelfth to thirteenth centuries, the few remaining **vestiges of the Temple of Venus of Eryx** have been found. From the crest of the precipitous rock we can admire a splendid panorama sweeping from the Cape of San Vito to Trapani below with the Egadi islands as a background, to the salt-works and Lilybaean coast toward Marsala, and to Valderice. On especially clear days it is possible to make out the coast of Tunisia.

The **Pepoli Castle** is surrounded by the magnificent garden

called **Giardino del Balio**, and is built on the site of the ancient acropolis of Eryx.

The **'A. Cordici' City Museum** is in the Municipal Palace. Its collections consist of archaeological remains from prehistoric to Roman times (there is an important *Head of Aphrodite* of the fifth to fourth centuries B.C.) and paintings from the seventeenth to nineteenth centuries. There is, finally, an interesting collection of coins, and a marble *Annunciation* attributed to Antonello Gagini (first half of the sixteenth century).

The "Chiesa Matrice" with its powerful battlemented bell tower.

Some evocative views of the town with its little churches, the ring walls and a detail of the ancient stones which still pave the winding alleys of Erice.

56

The beach and the gulf from the picturesque town.

CASTELLAMARE DEL GOLFO

A pretty bathing centre in the middle of the gulf of the same name, with a distinctive setting and views. In ancient times it was probably Segesta's outlet to the sea; in the Middle Ages it belonged to Alcamo and was known as *Porto d'Alcamo*. The **Castle**, built in the fourteenth century, was considerably altered at a later date.

Nearby, at **Terme Segestane**, is a hot salt and sulphur spring, of which the mud and vapours are also used, and which is particularly recommended for arthropathies, arthritis and neuritis, rheumatism, skin complaints, metabolic diseases and problems of the respiratory tract.

West of Castellamare, along the picturesque coast of **Scopello**, we see the imposing shapes of the **Faraglioni** rocks rise from the sea, creating an exceptionally striking landscape.

ALCAMO

This town, known as the birthplace of the thirteenth century poet Ciullo (or Cielo) d'Alcamo, lies in a magnificent setting on the slopes of Mount Bonifato, with a scenic view of the Gulf of Castellamare. The town derives its name from the Arab 'Alqamah who founded it in the ninth century. In the Swabian period (thirteenth century) a new centre was formed lower down, at the foot of Mount Bonifato. From the following century on it was an Aragonese dominion, and later a

The fourteenth century castle and the seventeenth century
Church of the Collegio.

feud of various noble houses.

The **Chiesa Matrice** is a seventeenth century church named
after the Virgin of the Assumption. On the same site previously was a fourteenth century church, of which the portal and
the elegant bell tower remain. The interior has an aisled nave
and frescoes by Borremans in the apse and dome; it also contains works by Antonio Gagini, such as the *Death of the Virgin* (left aisle) and the *Crucifix* (right aisle), and others by his
pupils.

In the seventeenth century **Church of San Francesco** are a
marble altarpiece, considered probably to be the work of
Domenico Gagini, and two sculptures, representing the *Mag-
dalen* and *St. Mark*, attributed to Antonello Gagini.

The **Badia Nuova**, known also as the *Church of San Francesco di Paola* preserves a painting by P. Novelli and allegorical
decorations by G. Serpotta.

In the **Church of San Salvatore** *(Badia Grande)* are other canvases by Novelli and sculptures by Antonio Gagini. The
Church of Sant'Oliva (eighteenth century) has a painting by
Novelli (high altar) and works by the Gaginis, including a
figure of Saint Olive, attributed to Antonello.

The **Church of the Santi Paolo e Bartolomeo**, which has
characteristically Baroque traits, houses an admirable *Madonna del Miele* (Madonna of the Honey), by an unknown fourteenth century artist.

The **Castle** (fourteenth century) goes back to the Aragonese
period, and is square in plan with massive towers at the
angles.

A panorama and the ossuary monument to the battle of Calatafimi.

CALATAFIMI

This large country town in the upper Val di Mazara was founded before the Roman conquest, and developed during the Arab period around a fortress which gave its name to the locality. A feudal possession during the Middle Ages, it became famous during Garibaldi's Sicilian campaign, when an epic battle, decisive for the capture of Palermo, took place there (15th May 1860). The remains of the **Castle** (thirteenth century) are interesting, as are some Baroque churches. An **Ossuary Monument** recalls the battle between Garibaldi and the Bourbons.

But the most important sight-seeing place in this area is undoubtedly ancient **Segesta**.

This page and next, some views of the majestic fifth century B.C. Doric temple.

SEGESTA

This city, founded by the Elymians, was in perpetual conflict with Selinunte and was called by the Greek peoples Egesta. As an ally of the Carthiginians, it was besieged by the Syracusans who captured it toward the end of the fourth century B.C. After various vicissitudes it yielded to Rome (first half of the third century B.C.). The ancient city rose on the terraced slopes of Mount Barbaro and seems to have been gradually abandoned after the Roman conquest, being finally destroyed by the Vandals.

The **Temple** is one of the most significant examples extant of Doric architecture. Dating from the second half of the fifth century B.C., it rises outside the urban area, on a slope on the west side of Mount Barbaro. The temple building is among the best conserved in Italy. The Doric peristyle, never in fact completed, consists of robust archaic columns on a base with three high steps, supporting the powerful entablature; there are tympana in the frontons.

The **Theatre** rises in an evocative setting with an impressive view. Partly built into the hillside, it dates from the fourth to third centuries B.C. and has an auditorium of 20 levels of steps divided into seven blocks. Little is left of the stage, the walls of which were decorated with scenes connected with the god Pan.

In **Contrada Mango** have been found the substantial remains of an Elymian **Sanctuary** of the sixth to fifth century B.C.; some archaeological material has also been found here (pottery, inscriptions and graffiti), but is difficult to decipher and interpret.

Next pages, further views of the temple and the fourth-third century B.C. theatre.

The Baroque "Chiesa Madre".

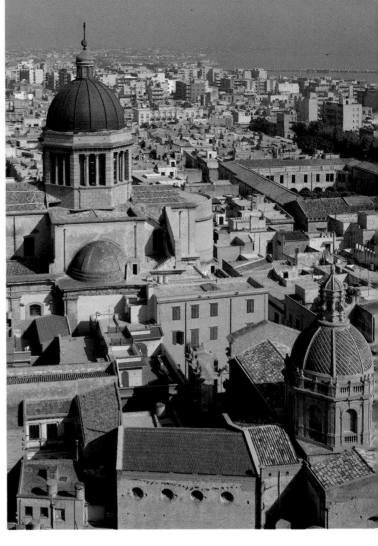

A view from the top of the historical centre.

*The third century B.C. remains of the Insula Romana and a ▶
floor mosaic with a Gorgon's head.*

MARSALA

Marsala is the town with the largest population in the province of Trapani. It lies on Cape Boeo, otherwise known as Cape *Lilybaeum*, at the westernmost tip of Sicily. The economy of the place is based mostly on wine-growing (strong, sweet Marsala wines are famous), commerce and a certain amount of industry. The place where the present town stands was probably a Sicanian site. At the beginning of the fourth century B.C. the Carthaginian *Lilybaeum* took the place of nearby Motye. Later a Roman possession and flourishing in the Middle Ages, the town derived its name from the Arab words *Marsa'Ali* (port of Ali). Taken over by the Normans in the twelfth century, it later passed to the House of Aragon; in the sixteenth century the importance of Marsala declined considerably as a consequence of the artificial earthing up of its port, which was done to defend the city against the constant attacks of pirates. Marsala and its commerce returned to their old splendour in the eighteenth century, when the English promoted activities and trade connected with wine production. The legendary Landing of the Thousand on the 11th May 1860 took place at Marsala.
The **Palazzo Comunale**, known also as the *Loggia*, is an elegant eighteenth century building; its facade is marked by the combination of the colonnaded portico on the upper storey and the arcade on the ground floor. In the centre of the facade rises a clock-tower.
The **Duomo** (Cathedral) is a seventeenth to eighteenth century building with an unfinished facade. The interior has an aisled nave and possesses various works from the workshop of the Gaginis. We should notice particularly a marble altarpiece in the chapel to the left of the presbytery attributed to Antonello Gagini. In the right transept we can see a fine painting by Riccio (end of the sixteenth century).
The **Lilibeo National Museum** has been set up in the Baglio Anselmi, formerly a wine factory. We can see there archaeologically valuable prehistoric materials, ancient tomb furniture, finds from Motye (especially important is the statue of a man, an original Greek marble from the fifth century B.C.), fragments from Roman times, mosaic decorations and Medieval objects.
The small **Church of San Giovanni** rises on the site of an Early Christian baptistery, believed to have been where the Sibyl of Lilybaeum lived. It is possible to visit the grotto below, where there are a well and a Roman mosaic.
The so-called **Insula Romana** is an area of great archaeological interest which has given up vestiges of the Roman period connected with vast rooms of the third century B.C. with abundant mosaic decorations and the remains of a small bath building. In this area and elsewhere the remains of original Carthaginian and Roman buildings have been excavated.
To the north-east of Marsala, on the **Island of San Pantaleo**, in the so-called *Stagnone*, are the ruins of the town now called **Mozia**. Ancient *Motye* was, with Palermo and Solunto, one of the main outposts of Phoenician colonization in Sicily (eighth century B.C.).

The canal port and the central Piazza Repubblica with the statue of St. Vitus.

MAZARA DEL VALLO

This small town looks on to the canal-harbour at the mouth of the Mazaro river. A flourishing wine-producing and fishing centre, it is one of the most active maritime and fishing ports in western Sicily. An ancient Phoenician harbour, it belonged for a long time to the sphere of Selinunte, until the arrival of the Carthaginians (fifth century B.C.) and, later, the Roman colonists. In the Middle Ages it was known as *Selinuntina* and became a flourishing centre under the Arabs and Normans.

The present appearance of the **Cathedral** (eleventh century) is the result of rebuilding in the late seventeenth century. In the facade, which has a powerful bell tower beside it, is the portal with the figure in relief of Count Roger on horseback (sixteenth century). The interior, which has an aisled nave, is rich in sculptural decorations: to be noted is the *Transfiguration* by Antonino Gagini in the apse, with ornaments and stuccoes by Ferraro. In the left transept is a *Christ Derided* by Marabitti and a statue of *St. Vincent*, the work of Antonello Gagini.

The **Church of Santa Caterina**, behind the Cathedral, has a statue of St. Catherine by Antonello Gagini.

In the central **Piazza della Repubblica**, which is enhanced by the facades of eighteenth century buildings, stands a *Statue of St. Vitus* in Baroque style by I. Marabitti (second half of the eighteenth century).

San Nicolò Regale is a small church whose origins go back to the Norman period (twelfth century). The unusual square structure is topped by battlements.

EGADI ISLANDS

This group of islands off the coast of Trapani has a common origin and geological affinities with Sicily, even if it resembles nearby Africa in climate and landscape. The archipelago, which has recently been equipped with excellent tourist facilities, hotel complexes and organized residences, consists of the islands of Favignana, Levanzo and Marettimo, and the rocks **Formica** and **Maraone**.

In ancient classical times the islands were called *Aegates*; during the Punic Wars they were the scene of the famous naval Battle of the Aegatian Islands where the Roman fleet defeated the Carthaginians (243 B.C.).

Favignana is the largest of the islands, and is situated in the lower part of the archipelago. The ancient *Aegusa* of the Romans, it has provided interesting archaeological information on the periods from prehistory up to the Punic age. The town of Favignana lies on the northern coast, on the slopes of Mount Santa Caterina, the highest rise in the island (314 meters).

Levanzo rises from the sea to the north of Favignana, opposite Trapani, and is the nearest to Sicily of the Egadi Islands. Its highest point is the Pizzo del Monaco (278 meters), while the town of Levanzo, which is also the harbour, is on the southern coast. The island, called *Phorbantia* by the Romans, is known for its important vestiges of the Palaeolithic and Neolithic ages.

Marettimo is the furthest from the mainland of the islands of the archipelago and is also the highest; the Pizzo Falcone, in fact, attains 884 metres. Already known in ancient times as *Hiera*, it was for a long time in the possession of the Arabs.

Favignana, the largest of the Egadi Islands, and the shore of Levanzo.

This and next pages, the remains of Temple C.

SELINUNTE

The recently founded Archaeological Park of Selinunte takes in a large part of the area of the municipality of Castelvetrano; the ruins of the ancient city of Selinunte are scattered between the Gaggera hill to the west and the so-called Collina Orientale (Eastern hill) to the east.

The original settlement was founded in the seventh century B.C. near the river Selinos (the present Modione), which gave its name to the new colony, founded by people from Megara Hyblaea. The city was in constant conflict with the Elymians who had one of their most important settlements at Segesta, and for a long time was at enmity with Carthage also. The Carthaginians, coming to the aid of the people of Segesta, laid siege to Selinunte (409 B.C.); the town was wrecked, a large number of its inhabitants were massacred, at least 5000 people from Selinunte were taken captive and the temples were left in ruins. Hermocrates of Syracuse tried in vain to reorganize the ancient city, which was abandoned in favour of the Acropolis, and thus spent the dark years of the Phoenician occupation, until it was completely destroyed by what was left of its own population to prevent it being conquered by Rome (241 B.C.). A devastating earthquake in the early

Middle Ages completed the work of destruction, doing further serious harm to the marvellous ancient buildings, which have since then been more and more exposed to deterioration and decay. During the obscure medieval period, even the memory of the ancient Greek city was lost; in Arab times it was known as *Casale degli Idoli*, and was rediscovered only in the second half of the sixteenth century, by Fasello. The first excavations were begun in the first half of last century, and provision has been made only in recent times for the definitive disposition of the very interesting archaeological area; the Park was founded and the Antiquarium set up (it is still being arranged).

On the **Acropolis** we find substantial vestiges of the **ring walls**, rebuilt under the Phoenicians, and the remains of the powerful fortifications for which Hermocrates was responsible. Further down we find the remains of a **sacred enclosure** and **houses** going back to Punic times.

The temples of Selinunte are identified by letters of the alphabet, since it has not been possible to decipher what divinities they were consecrated to.

There is little left of **Temple O**, originally a Doric peripteral temple which must have had six columns on its facade and fourteen on its sides. To the north of this are the remains of

SELINUNTE

0   200   400
meters

Temple M

SITE OF THE ANCIENT CITY

MANUZZA
TOWER

PARISI HOUSES

ANTIQUARIUM

Temple G

State highway 115

North Gate

Sanctuary of
Zeus Meilichios

Temple F

Sanctuary of the
Malophoros

Temple E

NECROPOLIS

Modione River

Gorgo di Cottone

Acropolis

Temple D
Temple C

NORTH

Temple B

BURIED PORT

BURIED PORT

State highway 115

Entrance

Via Marco Polo

Via G. Caboto

Temple A

Temple O

The ruins of Temple B and some views of the acropolis (sixth-fifth century B.C.).

another Doric peripteral temple, similar to the first but in a better state of repair. It is known as **Temple A**, and its altar has been found. Both these temples seem to date from the first half of the fifth century B.C. In this zone we see also the remains of a porticoed peripteral building of the same age as the temples, which must have served as a monumental entrance porch.

On the other side of the road which cuts across the Acropolis rise the ruins of **Temple B**, a small building perhaps dedicated to the cult of Aesculapius. It has four columns across its facade, and can be dated to the third to second centuries B.C. because the overlapping of Doric and Ionian styles that we observe in it is characteristic of the architecture of that period.

Nearby rise the colossal ruins of **Temple C**, the most ancient and grandest of the temples of Selinunte. It was founded in the first half of the sixth century B.C., and is a peripteral structure with six frontal columns, and with some of its columns and part of its entablature restored to their places in relatively recent times. In the metopes of the cella, which has a row of four columns in front, were true masterpieces of the sculptor's art; some of them can be seen at the Archaeological Museum in Palermo, where some other ornaments and clay fragments from the same temple are also kept. Nearby is what is left of **Temple D**, a Doric peripteral temple originally consisting of six columns across and thirteen on the sides, which was built in the second half of the sixth century B.C. The rest of the Acropolis, where we can see the remains of **houses** of the Punic period and **shops** and commercial zones, also possesses vestiges of **minor temples** which have given up important archaeological finds, such as the *Salinas Metope*, preserved in the Palermo museum.

At the top edge of the Acropolis, in the middle of some fortified structures of the Carthaginian period, is the **Northern Gate**. On the Eastern hill, perfectly aligned, are temples E, F and G.

Two views of Temple E (fifth century B.C.) possibly dedicated to the cult of Hera.

Pages 78-79, more views of Temple E and its cella. Pages 80-81, the imposing ruins of Temple G.

Temple G, the northernmost of the three, was certainly the most monumental and vast. It was begun in the second half of the sixth century B.C., but the Carthaginians destroyed the city before it could be finished. Although it is reduced today to a colossal heap of ruins, it has still been possible to reconstruct its plan exactly, and thus to conclude that it was one of the finest examples of Greek temple architecture. It was originally a pseudoperipteral structure with eight columns in front and seventeen on its long sides; inside was a cella, separated off by a double colonnade with ten columns each side and a pronaos with four columns in front. Theories as to the divinity possibly worshipped there are limited to Apollo and Olympian Zeus.

Temple F, the smallest of the three, dates from the middle of the sixth century B.C. and is surrounded by a peristyle with six columns at the ends and fourteen on each side. Inside was the cella with the pronaos and a further enclosed space. Of the many clay decorations that adorned the temple, only two metopes representing mythological motifs remain.

Further down the hill rises **Temple E**, the present appearance of which is the product of recent restoration, making very questionable use of modern building techniques. The original building was a Doric peripteral temple, with six columns in front and fifteen on the sides. It was built in the first half of the fifth century B.C., very probably on the site of an even more ancient construction. The cella, which is preceded by a pronaos, was decorated with metopes with mythological scenes, some of which are now on show in the Archaeological Museum in Palermo. Some interpretations suggest that the temple was consecrated to the cult of Hera.

On the Gaggera hill are the remains of the so-called **Sanctuary of the Malophoros**, one of the most famous and oldest sanctuaries of ancient Sicily, which seems to have been erected between the seventh and sixth centuries B.C. Its strange name refers to the cult of Demeter, the 'pomegranate-bearer', which was perhaps practised there. The ruins of the building stand inside a walled zone which enclosed the remains of various sacred areas.

To the north of this are the **Sanctuary of Zeus Meilichios** (the remains of a square enclosure) and **Temple M**, a rectangular structure of the sixth century B.C., probably a monumental fountain.

The South face of Temple E.

ISLAND OF PANTELLERIA

This island, the farthest out tip of Sicilian territory, is only 70 kilometres away from the coast of Tunisia. Already inhabited in the Neolithic period, it was conquered around the seventh century B.C. by the Pheonicians, who called it *Hirani*. Later disputed between Romans and Carthaginians, at the time of the Punic wars, it was won by the former, who changed its name to *Cossyra*. When Rome declined, it was the turn of the Vandals and the Byzantines, until the Arabs arrived. The Arab colonization left its mark in placenames and in the architectural styles still in use today.

The island, which was called by the Arabs *Bent el Rion*, was conquered by the Normans in the twelfth century. During the last World War it suffered violent bombing by the Allies.

The island is obviously of volcanic origin, and has the typical characteristics of secondary vulcanism. It is 836 metres high at the volcanic cone of Montagna Grande; and many other small craters can be seen, known locally as *cuddie*. Capers,

zibibbo grapes (the Pantelleria 'passito', wine made from dried grapes, is famous) and a growing tourist trade are the main items in the island's economy. Picturesque coasts, evocative inlets and natural caverns are the main attractions of this inviting island, where life goes on according to the rhythms of Mediterranean peasant culture, far from the hectic stress of modern daily life. The clear waters create a paradise for lovers of the sea and underwater fishing.

The most important places for sight-seers include the remains of a prehistoric settlement of the Neolithic period at *Mursia*, not far to the south of Pantelleria, which is the main town on the island, and grew up around the ancient **Barbacane Castle**, rebuilt in the eighteenth century. In the same area we can observe the distinctive **Sesi**, low round towers typical of megalithic funerary architecture.

Amongst the architectural curiosities of the place we must point out also the houses called **Dammusi**, built of stone with vaulted rooves. It is particularly enjoyable to make a tour of the island, either on the coastal road or by boat, in order to appreciate more fully its beautiful landscapes and fine views.

SCIACCA

An important place for tourists and health seekers on the coast of Agrigento, the little town of Sciacca spreads over hills sloping steeply to the sea. Its Hellenistic origins go back to the time of the colonization of Selinunte; the therapeutic properties of its thermal springs were recognized as early as the Roman period, when it was known as *Termae Selinuntinae*, and later as *Aquae Larodes*. In the Middle Ages it belonged first to the Arabs and then to the Normans, who reinforced its defense works.

The **Aragonese walls**, of which some stretches remain, go back to the sixteenth century.

The **Steripinto** is a sixteenth century building in Spanish plateresque style, with original diamond-point ashlar-work, battlements and lancet windows.

Close by, near the **San Salvatore Gate** (sixteenth century), is the **Church of the Carmine**, a building in Baroque style with a Gothic fronton on the facade.

On the opposite side of the street is the **Church of Santa Margherita**, originally built in the fourteenth century and remodelled in the sixteenth century. The portal on the facade looks Gothic; the one on the side is in Gothic-Renaissance style (fifteenth century) and is decorated with bas-reliefs by P. de Bonitate and F. Laurana. The stuccoes that adorn the interior are from the seventeenth century (O. Ferraro).

In the same street is the graceful **Casa Arone**, built in the fifteenth century, with elegant lancet windows in its facade. The **Duomo** was first built in the Norman period (twelfth century), but was completely altered in the eighteenth century. What is left of the original construction is the apse. On the facade and inside the Cathedral are many sculptures, some of which are the work of Antonello and Domenico Gagini. A Picture Gallery and a collection of coins have recently been arranged in the nearby **Casa Scaglione**.

On the way to the **Luna Castle**, a building of the second half of the fourteenth century of which only the walls and a cylindrical tower remain, is a small Romanesque (twelfth century) church called after **San Nicolò**, which has a facade with strong lines and three small apses at the back.

In the upper part of the town is the Piazza G. Noceto, where we find the sixteenth century **Church of San Michele** and the **San Calogero Gate**, opening on to what was the city perimeter in the sixteenth century.

On nearby **Mount San Calogero**, which looks down on the town from its height of 388 meters, are the **'Stufe di San Calogero'**, vents releasing radioactive steam that is utilized in therapy. The discovery of prehistoric material in the zone supports the hypothesis that the 'stufe' (ovens) were already in use in very ancient times.

At the top of the hill, in a very fine natural and panoramic situation, is the **Sanctuary of San Calogero**, which houses an admirable *Statue of St. Calogero* by G. Gagini (first half of the sixteenth century).

The San Salvatore gate (sixteenth century).

The sixteenth century Palazzo Steripinto.

Panorama of the port and town.   Aerial views of the islands of Lampedusa and Linosa. ▶

The Sciacca spa includes the **Nuove Terme** (New Baths), the **natural steam Stufe di San Calogero** and some hotels equipped for thermal therapy, including a recent establishment called **Sciaccamare**.

ISLAND OF LAMPEDUSA

The largest of the Pelagian islands is also the nearest Italian island to the coast of North Africa, and is 133 meters high at its highest point. The first human settlements there date from prehistoric times, which is demonstrated by findings from the Bronze Age and some megalithic constructions. Already known to the Romans (as *Lopadusa*) it was the scene of a naval battle between Arabs and Byzantines. For a long time it had no permanent inhabitants, but was settled again in the time of Ferdinand II. During the Second World War it was a centre for Allied military manoeuvres. In very recent

times it was touched by Libyan missiles during an acute international crisis.

Lampedusa lies on a harbour and is the only town worth mentioning; the sea coasts of the island are sheer cliffs and it is covered in typical Mediterranean scrub. The inhabitants are mostly employed in fishing, especially for sponges. Agriculture is made very difficult by lack of water.

ISLAND OF LINOSA

This is the first island we come to in the Straits of Sicily, and constitutes, together with Lampedusa and the desert rock Lampione, the Pelagian archipelago proper. Known in ancient times as *Aetusa (Algusa)*, it is obviously of volcanic origin. Its highest hill, Mount Vulcano, measures 195 meters. The only town of any size is **Linosa**, a typical agricultural and fishing settlement.

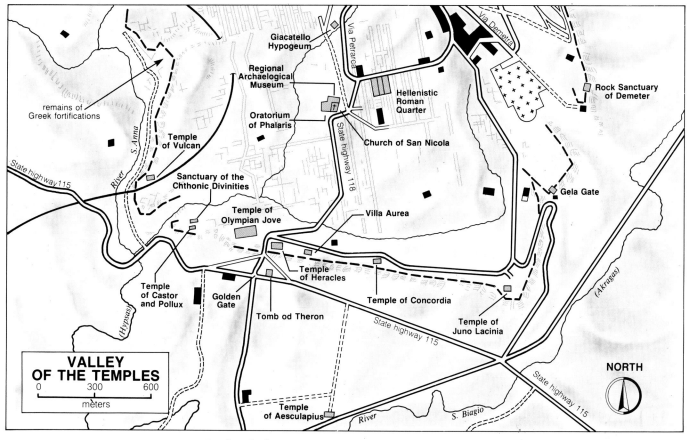

NORTH

◄ *What remains of the temple of Castor and Pollux, built in the fifth century B.C.*

AGRIGENTO

Historical Note. The city rises on the slopes of a mountain plateau bounded by the basins of the Sant'Anna river (the ancient *Hypsas*) and the San Biagio river (the ancient *Akragas*), in an evocative natural setting overlooking the panoramic Valley of the Temples and with the southern coast of the island visible in the distance. It is believed to have been founded by colonists coming from the Greek islands under an understanding with the inhabitants of nearby Gela (sixth century B.C.) In a short time *Akragas* grew in riches and power; under the Tyrant Theron it won a battle at Himera (fifth century B.C.) against a much larger Carthaginian army. The Carthaginians had their revenge toward the end of the century; the city gave in to hunger after a long siege, and was taken and laid waste. Rebuilt and repopulated by Timoleon, it was a bone of contention between Romans and Carthaginians until the former took firm possession of it, in 210 B.C. Under Roman protection *Agrigentum* enjoyed a period of calm and prosperity. Relentless decadence set in under the Byzantines. Having become an Arab possession in the first half of the ninth century, it changed its name to *Girgenti*, which it retained until 1927 when its present name was introduced. In the Swabian period it followed the fortunes of Palermo; in the fourteenth century it was subjected by the powerful house of Chiaramonte, from which it got free only toward the end of the century. Under the Aragonese it enjoyed customs exemptions which favoured its already prosperous commercial development. In the second half of the nineteenth century, its inhabitants distinguished themselves in the struggle for freedom from the Bourbon yoke. Outstanding people who were born at Agrigento include the philosopher Empedocles (fifth century B.C.) and the playwright Luigi Pirandello (1867-1936). With its favourable climate, mild even at the height of the cold season, and its exceptionally fine natural setting and views, it is one of the most popular tourist resorts in Sicily, an internationally celebrated archaeological, architectural and artistic centre. In early Spring the spectacular blossoming of the almond trees clothes the Valley of the Temples in a veil of strange and evocative beauty, and is the inspiration for the *Sagra del Mandorlo in Fiore* (Fair of the Almond in Flower), which is celebrated with a colourful array of local costumes and folklore and attracts enthusiastic crowds of Italian and especially foreign tourists. Among other festivities are further religious celebrations and the Pirandello festival in the Summer. The Via Atenea is the hub of the life of the town, the place where the people of Agrigento meet and prefer to stroll at sunset. Among the most characteristic craft articles on sale we find the 'scacciapensieri' (Jew's harp, or literally 'thought-chaser'), the typically Sicilian musical instrument played with the mouth, called locally *gargamarruni*. The weekly market of the itinerant vendors is held near the sports' fields, every Friday. It is impossible to describe the tourist spots and monuments of Agrigento without taking into consideration the configuration of the terrain and the layout of the city, which impose a division between the medieval and modern quarters and the ancient city proper (Valley of the Temples).

*Above, a view of the ruins of the Temple of Zeus;
(right), a view of the agora.*

◄ *Above, one of the colossal telamons that adorned the Temple
of Olympian Zeus, and, below, a capital from the temple.*

THE VALLEY OF THE TEMPLES

The exciting architectural remains of the ancient city are scattered over this valley, which is unique for the vastness of its views and the richness of its landscape, setting and monuments. The whole creates an intense Mediterranean vista, made almost fairylike by the play of colours, the intense scent of flowers and earth and the luminous presence of the sea which allays, with its constant breezes, the fierce rays of the Sicilian sun. From December to March the flowering of the almonds gives the place the appearance of a enchanted dream, celebrated with fairs and popular festivities. The temple zone can be reached by car from the state highroad and on foot from the Piazza Marconi in the centre of town.

Two views of the eight remaining columns of the Temple of Hercules.

Hellenistic-Roman Quarter:- This is a quite large section of an ancient town, settled in the fourth to third centuries B.C.; its most recent buildings date from the fourth to fifth centuries A.D.. Roads running in the four main directions form a grid on which stand the ancient houses, shops and other buildings. Some decorative mosaic floors have been preserved, together with stretches of intonacoed wall with paintings on them. The type of decoration gives us an idea of the dates of the extensive ruins, which stretch from the Republican to the Imperial periods (first, second and third century A.D.). Over the whole vast area we can see the remains of sewerage and water pipes. In this ancient residential area, there are three blocks and a few separate houses we may wish to see in particular. These include the *House of the Aphrodites, House of the Diamond Mosaic, House of the Peristyle* (a typical example of a luxurious home with attached baths), *House of the Gazelle* (which takes its name from the gazelle represented in the floor mosaics, now in the Museum), *House of the Abstract Master*, rich in admirable mosaics, and the *House of the Portico*.

Giacatello Hypogeum:- This is reached by a small road starting from the Archaeological Museum and following the stream of the same name. It is very probably an ancient (fifth century B.C.) water reservoir; its appearance today is that of a vast underground room like a square cistern, with skylights and a lining of beaten earth.

Church of San Nicola:- This building as we see it today goes back to the thirteenth century; it was built by the Cistercians on a site where there were the remains of ancient Greek and Roman buildings and where monastic communities had settled and built a first church dedicated to St. Nicholas. The church, between Romanesque and Gothic in style, has a fine portal in the facade; the *interior* has a single nave. It contains a Greek sarcophagus with carvings representing the *myth of Phaedra*, held to be a Roman work of the second to third centuries A.D. and once kept in the Aula Capitolare of the Cathedral. We should particularly note the apse, which is distinguished for its row of little blind arches of Romanesque type and powerful stone ogival vault.

◄ *The small funerary monument called Tomb of Theron (first century B.C.).*

◄ *The ruins of the Temple of Aesculapius.*

This and next pages, some views of the Temple of Concordia, built around the fifth century B.C., the best preserved of all the temples in Sicily.

Close by, near the remains of a theatre building dug out of the rock, is the **Oratory of Phalaris**, a temple building with a small hexedra rising on a podium.

Temple of Hercules:- Among the ruins of this temple stand the eight columns raised again, in 1924, out of the 44 that adorned the building. It is a Doric temple, almost certainly the most ancient of the temples of Agrigento, and dates from the sixth century B.C. It is distinguished for the originality of its structure, of which three of the tall steps bounding the rectangular platform remain.
The *Herakleion* was originally a peripteral temple with six columns; its cornice, originally of clay, was later replaced by one in stone, decorated with lion heads and considerably restored during Roman times. In the westernmost zone of the excavations we find the **Tomb of Theron**, of the Roman period (first century B.C.), near the ancient **Porta Aurea** (Golden Gate) in a beautiful landscape setting, and the remains of the ancient **Temple of Aesculapius** (fifth century B.C.), the style of which is pure Doric.

Temple of Olympian Zeus:- Many visible vestiges remain of the ancient temple of Zeus (Jupiter), built in the fifth century B.C. to celebrate the victory of the Carthaginians at Himera.

The building, attacked by repeated earthquakes and almost entirely razed by the Carthaginians at the end of the fifth century B.C., was despoiled right up to the end of the seventeenth century for materials to be used in buildings and public works.
The *Olympeion* was a pseudo-peripteral temple which had, instead of a peristyle, a powerful wall with semi-columns at intervals where the giant figures of the *Telamons* stood. These figures had the function of helping to support the massive structure of the entablature; a copy of one of them, restored, can be seen on the ground in the temple, while the original has been transferred to the Archaeological Museum. In ancient times this temple was believed to be second in size only to the Cyclopean Temple of Diana at Ephesus.

Temple of Castor and Pollux:- The four columns which for a long time have been the emblem of Agrigento stand as we see them today thanks to the restoration carried out last century by the sculptor V. Villareale and the architect S. Cavallari. They are all that is left of a temple built in the fifth century B.C., and are marked by the admirable decoration of the architraves, in Hellenistic-Roman style.
In this area have also been found the remains of religious buildings and very ancient sanctuaries (going back as far as

Three views of the Temple of Juno Lacinia, built around the middle of the fifth century B.C.

the sixth century B.C.), dedicated to Demeter and Persephone and known as a whole as the **Sanctuary of the Cthonic Divinities**.

In the western part of the Valley of the Temples are the ruins of the **Temple of Vulcan**, a Doric building dating from the fifth century B.C.

Temple of Concordia:- To reach this temple we pass by the **Villa Aurea** (in the direction of the excavations), near which are the **Roman necropolis of Giambertoni** (second century B.C. to fourth century A.D.), the remains of a Byzantine necropolis and the catacombs called **Grotta di Fragapane** (fourth century A.D.).

A splendid example of Doric architecture, and one of the greatest attractions and archaeological treasures in Sicily, the temple has come down to us in an excellent state of conservation, although the wear of centuries has eroded the structure of the shell-limestone tufa of which it is built and stripped it of its stucco coating.

The building, which is similar in structure and colour to the Temple of Theseus at Athens, was originally dedicated to Castor and Pollux and built, in all probability, in the time of Theron (fifth century B.C.). It is a hexastyle peripteral temple with 34 columns standing on a platform with four steps up to it. It was converted into a Christian basilica in the sixth century; the arched openings in the walls of the cella are of that period.

◄ *The archaeological remains of the Greco-Roman quarter.*

◄ *The early Christian necropolis.*

A room in the Archaeological Museum where one of the telamons from the Temple of Olympian Jove can be admired.

Temple of Juno Lacinia:- This also is a hexastyle peripteral temple in pure Doric mould; it is the best preserved of the temples of Agrigento after the Temple of Concordia. Built around the middle of the fifth century B.C., it was soon after damaged by a fire which led to its restoration in Roman times. Of the original building 25 columns are left, some of them truncated. Particularly imposing is the colonnade on the north side supporting the powerful architrave.

Rock Sanctuary of Demeter:- This very ancient building, dug out of the rock around the seventh century B.C., dates from before the Greek civilization; it overlooks an area rich in **fortifications** erected by the Greeks, below which is the ancient **Gela Gate**, where objects connected with the cult of the Cthonic Divinities have been found. Uphill from the Sanctuary of Demeter is a fifth century **Doric temple** also dedicated to her; in medieval times it was converted into a church dedicated to San Biagio.

Regional Archaeological Museum:- Counted among the biggest and best arranged museum collections of this kind in Sicily, the Archaeological Museum of Agrigento exhibits important finds from the town and from other zones nearby.
In **Room I** we find information of topographical and cartographical interest on the ancient settlement of Agrigento and materials from classical times.
Room II displays finds from prehistoric times, especially the Aeneolithic period and the Bronze and Iron Ages, and materials from Gela, the necropolis of Montelusa and other necro-

polises in the region, dating from the seventh to sixth centuries B.C.
In **Room III** is a valuable collection of pottery from the fifth to third centuries B.C., among which the typical Attic vases and the Greek-Italiot vases stand out. Of particular interest is the crater with a representation of the myth of *Perseus and Andromeda* on it (fifth century B.C.).
In **Room IV** we can see interesting fragments of temples, stone water spouts with lion heads and other ornaments.
Room V brings together materials from the Agrigento temple complex, including admirable sculptures from the Greek, Hellenistic and Siceliot periods.
In **Room VI**, which is dedicated to the Temple of Olympian Zeus, the most important item is the reconstruction, out of the original materials, of the gigantic *Telamon* (about eight metres) which once stood in the temple; it was one of a series and the heads from some of the others can also be seen in this room.
In **Room VII** we find interesting materials from the Hellenistic-Roman quarter, especially the *emblemata* from the mosaic floors that adorned some of the buildings.
Room VIII contains a collection of inscriptions, where we notice especially those from Agrigento monuments of the Greek age.
In **Room IX** (after obtaining permission to enter) we can see gold, silver and bronze coins from the classical to medieval periods. Most noteworthy are the silver Agrigentum coins of the fifth century B.C., with interesting figures on them.
Room X contains an admirable marble sculpture of an Ephe-

bus, a Greek original of the fifth century B.C.

In **Room XI** are finds from the ancient necropolises in the Agrigento area.

Rooms XII-XIII display prehistoric finds and materials from the necropolises and excavation zones in the province and bordering regions. The most important are those from the Agrigento necropolis of Sant'Angelo Muxaro.

Room XIV contains material of topographical interest from some centres round Agrigento.

Room XV contains a variety of materials from Gela, among which we note particularly an original Greek crater from the fifth century B.C. with red figures representing the *Battle of the Amazons*.

Rooms XVI-XVII contain finds from the necropolises and the ancient Nissene settlements, with topographically interesting representations of the province of Caltanissetta.

Room XVIII (which can be visited by permission) houses the so-called **Museo di Seconda Scelta** (Second Choice Museum).

In **Room XIX** (which has a separate entrance) temporary exhibitions are held.

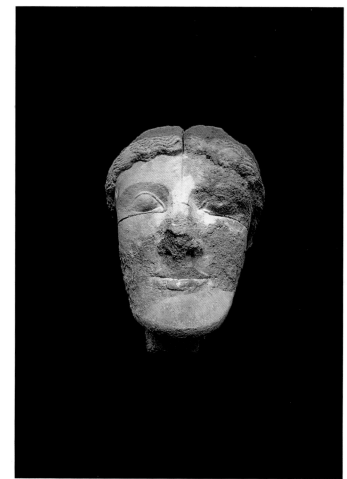

◄ *Archaeological Museum: some Greek vases from the outstanding collection; a splendid marble torso from the fifth century B.C., the head of a man (Hercules) in marble, and the statue of an Ephebus, probably the work of a sculpture from Agrigento (470 B.C.).*

Archaeological Museum: the head of a telamon from the Temple of Olympian Zeus and a fragment of a Roman mosaic.

Three snapshots of Luigi Pirandello: as a highschool student (1885), as a university student at Palermo (1887), and the last photo of him.

The house where Luigi Pirandello was born. ►

The writer's ashes rest in the limestone block at ► the foot of the "solitary pine".

Luigi Pirandello

The Sicilian writer and playwright Luigi Pirandello is considered one of the most important representatives of literary and theatrical culture at the turn of the century. Born at Girgenti in 1867, he went to school in Palermo where he subsequently enrolled in university courses in the faculties of Law and Letters. He moved to Rome, continued his studies in the humanities and published a collection of poems (*Mal Giocondo*, 1889). Having graduated in Glottology in Germany, he returned to Rome, and wrote the poems in the collection *Amori senza Amore*, a prelude to his great story-writing activity which produced the *Novelle per un anno* (1922-1936). *L'Esclusa* (1925), and even more his following works (*Il Fu Mattia Pascal*, 1904; *Così è se vi pare*, 1918; *Uno, nessuno, centomila*, 1926) establish the qualities of Pirandello's prose, a curious mixture of realistic experiences and tormented intuitions about the meaninglessness of life. Between 1918 and 1927 Pirandello wrote plays such as *Il gioco delle parti*, *Ma non è una cosa seria* and above all the well known *Sei personaggi in cerca di autore* ("Six Character in Search of an Author"). The founding of the Teatro d'Arte in Rome (1925) and the reception of the Nobel Prize for literature (1934) were milestones in the career of this great playwright, who died in Rome in 1936.

The ruins of the ancient monastery and the remains of the cloister of the Church of the Carmine.

PALMA DI MONTECHIARO

This town lies on the lower slopes of Mount Pozzillo, near the coast. Ancient finds from a cave near the place demonstrate that human beings lived there already in prehistoric times. A distinguishing feature of the town is that it was built in the seventeenth century by Carlo Tomasi di Lampedusa, an ancestor of Giuseppe, author of the novel *The Leopard*. The **Chiesa Madre** has a certain interest; it has Baroque traits, as do some other buildings.

On the nearby **Marina** we can seen the **Castle of the Princes of Lampedusa**.

Near the town, high up on a rock overlooking the sea, rises the **Castle of Montechiaro** (fourteenth century).

Also in the surroundings are the seventeenth century **Fortress of San Carlo** and the fifteenth century **Castellazzo di Palma**.

CALTANISSETTA

Historical Note:- The city lies in the upper part of the Valle del Salso, on the southern slopes of Mount San Giuliano, which is the geometrical centre of Sicily. Its origins are remote, and seem to date from a period earlier than the Classical age, when a *Nissa* is heard of. The Saracens added the prefix *Kalat*, and the placename acquired the strange meaning of "castle of women".

The town is surrounded by a fertile agricultural district and is the centre of Sicilian mining territory. The mines were very active in the thirties, but although they still produce a considerable quantity of sulphur and of potassium and manganese salts, they have declined now that new sources of energy have been found.

Duomo:- The Cathedral was begun in the second half of the sixteenth century and finished in the first half of the following century. The *facade*, which is quite wide, is in two tiers, adorned by pilasters and framed between two bell towers, and goes back to the first half of last century.

The *interior*, sumptuous and solemn, has marked eighteenth century rococo traits. There are many stuccoes which provide a florid frame for the numerous frescoes by the Flemish artist Guglielmo Borremans.

The Church of San Sebastiano.

The interior of the Baroque Cathedral.

GELA

An important industrial and commercial town, Gela stands at the mouth of the river of the same name, on the southern coast of Sicily. The town is developing as a bathing resort for tourists, and is also known because of the ANIC petrochemical complex there. Already settled in prehistoric times, it is a city of Doric origin, founded by settlers from Rhodes and Crete (seventh century B.C.). Devastated in the fifth century B.C. by the Carthaginian militia, it was rebuilt a century later by Timoleon. In the third century B.C. the city was razed by the Mamertines and fell into oblivion until the first half of the thirteenth century when, under Frederick II, it rose again as *Terranova*. It got its old name back only in 1928. On Good Friday a picturesque *Crucifixion* pageant is held there.

In the eastern part of the town, on the site of the ancient acropolis, the remains of the **Timoleon Quarter** have been brought to light. They date from the fourth century B.C.; below them are traces of even more ancient constructions. In the **Parco della Rimembranza** below, we can see the base and the ruins of a *Doric temple* of the fifth century B.C. and the more ancient *Temple of Athena* (sixth century B.C.). This was probably a peripteral structure, but little is left of it besides the base; the fine clay ornaments found on the site were taken to the Syracuse Museum. From the nearby look-out point we can admire a wide panorama of the plain of Gela. Also in the same area is the **Archaeological Museum**, the various sections of which display valuable archaeological finds from this district and surrounding districts. In the first section, where we find material from the prehistoric and archaic periods, the most interesting item is the fifth century *terracotta horse head*. In the second section are finds from sanctuaries in the area and from the acropolis; a clay statuette of *Demeter* and statuettes of *Athena seated* stand out among the rest. The third section contains finds from ancient settlements outside the town, sanctuaries outside the acropolis and ancient ceramic objects and fragments (seventh to fourth centuries B.C.). In the fourth section are materials connected with the city, from the fourth to third centuries B.C., finds from Cape Soprano, inscriptions and ancient ceramic graffiti (sixth to fifth centuries B.C.). The fifth section displays items from sanctuaries outside the walls and ancient earthenware vases dating from the fifth century B.C. In the same section are funerary objects from the ancient Greek necropolises. The seventh section consists of materials from Gela and its surroundings. The eighth section provides a glimpse of the city in the Early Christian and Medieval ages. In the ninth section are private collections, terracottas and vases of Attic origin. The museum also contains a fine *numismatic collection* with Siceliot and Athenian coins.

The eighteenth century "Chiesa Matrice".

The Park of Remembrance and excavation in the fourth ▶
century B.C. archaeological zone.

Further important vestiges of the ancient city can be seen at **Cape Soprano**, where quite well preserved remains of **fortifications** dating from the fifth and fourth centuries B.C. are scattered. These fortificatons were restored at the time when Timoleon rebuilt the town in the fourth century B.C., and consist of blocks of stone below with unbaked bricks above. From the way the ruins lie it is possible to deduce the original layout of the complex, which included a number of towers alternating with sentry beats.

Not far away are the remains of the **Greek baths** (fourth century B.C.) where we can see clearly the arrangement of the bathing pools and the system used to heat the water.

The **Chiesa Matrice** on Piazza Umberto I in the centre of town is worth seeing; it is an eighteenth century building with a facade in Neo-Classical style.

To the north of Gela is the **Lago del Disueri**, an artificial basin built to irrigate the plain below. On the outcrops above it "oven" type Sicilian tombs have been found that once belonged to an extensive prehistoric necropolis.

Ancient ruins, dating from the fourth century B.C. and belonging to a settlement of indigenous people, have come to light on nearby **Mount Bubonia**.

Regional Archaeological Museum: a vase with the scene of ▶
Theseus killing the Minotaur (470-460 B.C.); a statuette from the acropolis of Gela and an antefix from Sila in terracotta (fifth century B.C.).

Regional Archaeological Museum: a black-figure vase from the acropolis of Gela; the superb fifth century B.C. horse's head; a Gorgon's head antefix.

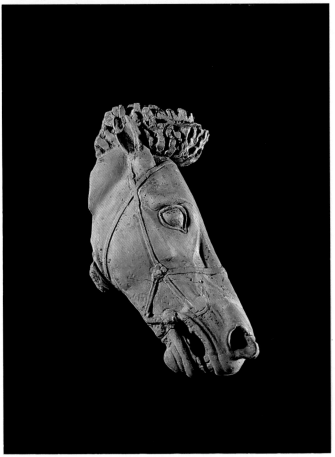

ENNA

Historical Note:- The city competes with nearby Caltanissetta to be considered the geometrical centre of Sicily. Because of its central position on the island it was called even in ancient times the *Navel of Sicily*. Of very ancient origin, *Henna* was a Sicanian centre where a cult similar to that of Demeter developed. At the time of the Greek colonization, the city succeeded in retaining a certain autonomy, which was challenged first by Agathocles of Syracuse (fourth century B.C.) and then by Carthage. It became a Roman possession and paid back with severe repression the slave revolt that occurred in the second century B.C. A *municipium* during the Imperial age, it was conquered by the Byzantines on the decline of Roman power. Because of its strategic position, which made it practically impregnable, it resisted the Arabs for a long time, and was occupied by them only after a siege lasting more than twenty years, in 859. Named by its new rulers *Kasrlanna*, the city went through a period of prosperity which lasted until the advent of the Normans (eleventh century). In following centuries, now called *Castrum Iohannis*, it became a possession of Angevins and Aragonese, according to the vicissitudes of Sicilian history.
The Enna of our time rises at the top of a terraced mountain spur, a highly panoramic setting in the middle of an agricultural district where mining activities also prosper. Over the last ten years its tourist trade has become substantial.

Duomo:- The Cathedral dates from the fourteenth century, having been built in the middle of the Aragonese period. Seriously damaged by fire in the second half of the fifteenth century, it was rebuilt in the Baroque age (seventeenth century). The powerful *facade* looks on to a sweeping flight of steps and has a porch with a seventeenth century tower above it. The apse is in three parts and in Gothic style.
The dramatic *interior* has a nave and two aisles divided by powerful pillars supporting ogival arches. In the left aisle we observe the sixteenth century *holy-water stoup*, the *pulpit* carved by G. Gallina (seventeenth century), and the admirable baptismal font. The coffered wooden ceiling is also worth noting.

Castello di Lombardia:- This ancient building in the highest part of the town was probably built earlier than the Swabian period, when it is usually held to have originated.
Only six towers remain of the twenty that once existed; one of the most important is the *Pisan Tower*, which is crowned by a battlemented structure.

Torre di Federico:- This strange, octagonal structure rises in the middle of the public gardens and dates from the thirteenth century, when it was probably part of a larger and more important castle.

The imposing ''Castello Lombardia'', the tower of Frederick II, ▶
and a panorama of Caltanissetta.

The facade and the apse of the Cathedral.

A view of the town.

The bell tower of the Cathedral, the eighteenth century ▶
Palazzo di Città and the ancient Church of the Commenda
(twelfth century).

Thursday, March 16, 2000

PIAZZA ARMERINA

Although it is situated inland, Piazza Armerina is one of Sicily's most important tourist resorts. It lies along a ridge in the Erei mountains, in a setting of great natural beauty and near an area which has great archaeological interest because one of the finest Roman villas that have come down to us still stands there. Once known as *Platia*, it developed as a marketplace where the Lombard militia spent their money, which would explain its strange name. According to some sources it already existed before the Roman colonization, when it was known as *Hibla*. In the Middle Ages it suffered various vicissitudes, including being destroyed in the second half of the twelfth century by William the Bad. Later, Piazza Armerina competed for a long time with Enna to become the Bishop's See, succeeding in this only in the first half of the nineteenth century. The *Palio dei Normanni*, which is held in August, is the most important of the folk festivities of the town.

The powerful outline of the **Duomo** is the first sight we have of the town on approaching. A building with Baroque characteristics, it goes back to the seventeenth century and was built over a previous fifteenth century church. The facade overlooks a flight of steps and has sixteenth century Mannerist features and a strange portal adorned with spiral tufa columns in Renaissance taste. The attached bell tower has Catalan Gothic traits and belonged to the old fifteenth century building. The magnificent Baroque interior is crowned by a spectacular dome; on the high altar is a precious silver tabernacle with a splendid Byzantine painting of the *Holy Virgin of Victory*, while on the side walls are sixteenth century paintings by Zoppo di Gangi. An admirable arch attributed to A. Gagini to the right of the entrance contains the *baptismal font*. In the chapel on the left is a fine wooden *Crucifix* attributed to the Maestro della Croce di Piazza Armerina (fifteenth century), together with a fifteenth century *Madonna and Child*, of Umbrian origin. Paintings in the church include works by F. Paladino, G. Martorana and J. Ligozzi. In the attached **Cathedral Museum** we can see fine bas-reliefs, precious reli-

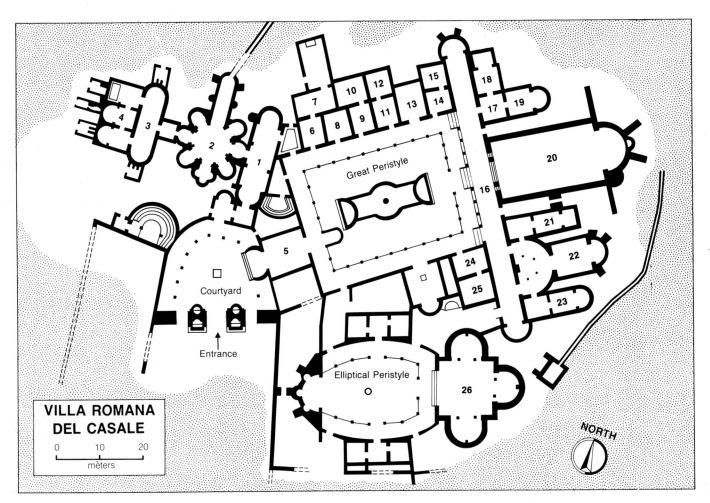

VILLA ROMANA
DEL CASALE

0   10   20
mèters

LEGEND

1. Gymnasium
2. Frigidarium
3. Tepidarium
4. Calidarium
5. Atrium
6. Room in Norman bakery
7. Inner room
8. Room with geometrical star mosaic
9. Room of lost mosaic
10. Room of the Dance
11. Room of the Seasons
12. Room of the "Amorini" Fishing
13. Room of the Little Hunt
14. Room with octagon mosaic
15. Room with check mosaic
16. Ambulacrum with mosaics of the Great Hunte
17. Vestibule of Polypemus
18. Cubiculum with erotic scene
19. Cubiculum with fruit decorations
20. Basilica
21. Cubiculum of the Boy Hunters
22. Room of Arion
23. Cubiculum with chorus and actors
24. Room with panel mosaics
25. Room of the Ten Girls
26. Triclinium

*The Roman villa at Casale, built between the third and fourth ►
centuries A.D.*

The octagonal room of the "frigidarium". ►

*Pages 118-119, a scene from the mosaic of the gymnasium: a
trumpet player signals the end of the race, while a magistrate
presents the palm of victory; and the details of the chariot
and the trumpet player.*

quiaries, silver objects and ancient Christmas cribs.
The **Church of the Gran Priorato di Sant'Andrea** is from the
twelfth century and is counted among the most ancient
churches in the town. It has the distinctive features of
medieval architecture, including a portal with Arab and Norman stylistic motifs.
Among other churches worth noting, we find the seventeenth
century **Church of Fundrò**, which has a fine tufa portal with
Baroque decorations, the ancient Gothic **Church of the Commenda** (twelfth century), once seat of the *Order of the
Knights of Jerusalem and Malta*, the seventeenth century
Church of Santo Stefano and the **Church of San Pietro**
(seventeenth century), which has sculptures from the workshop of the Gagini and an eighteenth century wooden
ceiling.
The **Aragonese Castle** was built during the fourteenth century

A detail of the mosaic in the antechamber of the baths: a matron accompanied by servants on her way to the baths.

"Corridor of the Great Hunt": detail of the embarkation of the ►
animals destined for the Circus.

Next pages, other scenes from the "Corridor of the Great Hunt": the owner of the villa with his officials and the capture of a stag. Scenes from the "Room of the Ten Girls": young girls in scant costumes playing gymnastic games.

under Martin I of Aragon; it is a structure with a square base and corner towers, which stands out among the buildings of the town.

We must mention, finally, the **Palazzo Trigona** (eighteenth century), which has both Renaissance and Baroque features, and the so-called **Palazzo di Città** (City Palace), an eighteenth century edifice built as a Benedictine monastery, in which we can admire frescoes by G. Martorana.

The **Roman Villa of Casale** remains, however, the most important sight to see in the region, and is one of the finest examples of Roman country dwellings on the island. It was built in the third-fourth century B.C., and its happiest time was between the fourth and fifth centuries A.D., just before the devastations wrought by the barbarians. The splendour of the

mosaic decorations in the floors has made this ancient Roman villa famous all over the world. It was brought to light in the late twenties, and the work of excavating it is not yet complete. The wide use of mosaics to beautify the floors and walls of the extraordinary complex gives us an important insight into mosaic technique; the work was very probably done by artists of North African origin, and is one of the finest examples existing of this type of decoration, widely used by the Romans wherever they went.

The entrance leads to an **Atrium** of poligonal plan with a colonnade, a fountain in the centre and stretches of mosaic paving. We continue through the **Vestibule**, which has a fine mosaic in its floor, and come to the **Big Peristyle**, with a marble colonnade, a pool in the centre and numerous mosaic

"Fishing Room": "amorini" casting their fishing nets.

Private apartments: scene from the "Little Circus" with a boy ▶
charioteer; a boy playing with a swan on a leash.

Room with apse: Neptune, a detail of the legend ▶
of Arion of Lesbos.

decorations, which are a feature also of the rooms on the north side. Among these last the scene of the *Little hunt* is famous. The long **Ambulacrum of the great hunt** is rich in mosaic scenes celebrating the hunting and capture of wild animals. On the lower side of the Big Peristyle is the room with the well known scene of *Women gymnasts*. Known also as the **Room of the Ten Girls**, it attracts our attention with its figures of young girls, dressed in scanty costumes (comparable to the modern bikini), playing gymnastic games.

In an adjacent room with a fountain in the middle is a scene with *Orpheus*. On the east side of the Ambulacrum of the great hunt is a room similar to a basilica with an apse where company must have been received. To the south of this was the part of the house used for living in, also rich in fine

mosaic decorations. Scenes with mythological subjects adorn also the rooms on the east side of the upper part of the already mentioned Ambulacrum. Coming to the **Elliptical Peristyle**, a courtyard with a portico and fountain in the centre, we can see the mosaics in the rooms that open on to it, which represent "Amorini" intent on fishing and picking grapes. We then come to the **Triclinium**, an interesting room with three apses and mosaics with mythological scenes. Returning to the Atrium, we come to the **Salone del Circo** (Hall of the Circus), so called for its mosaics, which represent scenes of competitions in the Circus Maximus in Rome. We then go on to the baths, where we can distinguish the different rooms, the **Frigidarium**, the **Tepidarium** and the **Calidarium**, and their respective heating systems.

Some views of the excavations of the pre-Hellenistic city.

MORGANTINA

The big village of Aidone is situated in a beautiful natural setting, with a fine view, on the slopes of the Erei mountains, not far from Piazza Armerina. It developed during the Arab period, in a previously settled area, and is known through the history of its castle, which from the Norman age on came under the control of various feudal lords.

Of great interest is the **Antiquarium** which has been set up in a building which was once a Capuchin monastery. Materials found in nearby **Morgantina** are exhibited there. Morgantina is a very important archaeological zone, discovered in the fifties in the locality of Serra d'Orlando. Probably founded by Chalcidian colonists from Catania in the sixth century B.C., it was important in the Hellenistic and Roman periods, but went into a rapid and definitive decline in the first century B.C.

What has been brought to light of the ancient settlement is the **Agora**, which was built on two levels and included the **Macellum**, a Roman shopping centre, the **Bouleuterion**, the **Gymnasium**, the **Theatre**, the remains of rich houses with mosaic decorations, vestiges of a **Sanctuary** dedicated to the cult of the gods of the underworld, and a building used as a granary. The whole surrounding zone is scattered with ruins and partially buried remains, such as those of the **Sanctuary of Demeter and Kore**. On a nearby hill, traces of the ancient acropolis and a settlement devastated in the fifth century B.C. have been found.

A view of the city from above.

RAGUSA

Historical Note:- This town rises on the southern spurs of the Hyblaean (Ibla) Hills, in a region marked by the complexity of its system of river valleys, which constrict the towns of *Ragusa* and *Ibla* between the depressions dug out by the San Leonardo and San Domenico streams, tributaries of the Irminio catchment basin. Archaeological studies and the existence of ancient tombs dug into the rock support the theory that the place has been inhabited since prehistoric times, to be exact since the Bronze Age. This was certainly the site of the Sicel town known as *Hybla Heraea*, which established relations with Greek settlers from Camarina, a centre founded by Syracuse. We have little information about the Roman *Hibla*, which was probably razed by the Vandals.
Rebuilt by Dalmatian colonists from Ragusa, who gave it the name of their native place (seventh century A.D.), it was fortified in the Byzantine age by a ring wall, in order to resist the frequent raids of Saracen pirates. In the first half of the ninth century Ragusa fell into Arab hands. With the coming of the Normans, in the eleventh century, it was made a county, and a century later its jurisdiction was extended to include Modica. It became a feud of the Chiaramontes, then passed into the hands of the Aragonese and the Henriquez. Seriously damaged by the earthquake of 1542 and almost destroyed by that of 1693, its buildings and layout were substantially transformed.
In 1865 an administrative unit with the name of *Ragusa Ibla* was formed, comprising the oldest part of the town, while the new part, called *Ragusa Superiore*, developed more and more.
The Ragusa of our own days consists of two quite separate urban centres. On the eastern spur rises *Ibla*, the layout and buildings of which obviously spring from a medieval matrix. To the west spreads *Ragusa*, which is modern in appearance and has wide streets laid out in a regular grid pattern.

Cathedral:- This a vigorous eighteenth century construction, named after St. John the Baptist; it stands on Piazza San Giovanni Battista, which is surrounded by a marble balustrade, in the newer part of the town.
The elegant ***facade*** is patterned across its width on two tiers; in the lower tier it is divided up by powerful columns with ornate capitals. To the sides of the main portal are small twin fluted columns, which support an architectural arrangement of Baroque character, loaded with sculptures. To one side of the facade rises the tall and graceful bell tower, which is topped by a spire. Over the crossing of the nave rises a cupola supported by a poligonal tambour.
The ***interior*** is of the basilica type, with an aisled nave; the aisles open on to a series of chapels from last century, adorned with artistic stuccoes. Behind the Cathedral stands the ***Casa Canonica***, interesting for the architectural elegance of its eighteenth century lines.

Church of Santa Maria delle Scale:- This church in the

The Cathedral with its Baroque portal and the Church of San Giorgio, built in 1738-1775.

easternmost part of Ragusa takes its name from the charming flight of steps leading up to the **Church of Santa Maria dell'Itria** (eighteenth century). Santa Maria delle Scale was originally erected in the fifteenth to sixteenth centuries and largely rebuilt after the earthquake of 1693, preserving some parts of the original building, including the bell tower, the portal and the remains of the pulpit. The *interior*, which has an aisled nave with Gothic and Renaissance characteristics, contains, on the second altar from the right in a chapel remodelled in the sixteenth century, a clay bas-relief of the first half of the same century representing the *Death of the Virgin*; it has the marks of the Gagini workshop.

Church of San Giorgio:- A masterpiece of eighteenth century Baroque, this church with its Neo-Classical dome dominates the Ibla quarter. The design for this building was drawn up by R. Gagliardi, and it was completed in 1775. The dramatic **facade** looks down on a flight of steps and is designed on three orders, with columns marking the divisions and sculptural and flower motifs as adornments. Counted among the finest religious buildings in this part of Sicily, its *interior* has a nave divided from the two aisles by pilasters.

Church of San Giuseppe:- This Ibla church is also distinguished for the ornateness of its Baroque **facade**, which recalls motifs already present in the church of San Giorgio. This one also is the work of the architect Gagliardi. The *interior*, which has an unusual elliptical plan, also shows typical eighteenth century traits. Among the art works we should note the sixteenth century figure of St. Joseph.

Palazzo Donnafugata:- One of the most noteworthy examples of eighteenth-nineteenth century architecture, this palace

131

contains the **Private collection of Barone Arezzo**. There are paintings attributed to Spagnoletto and Caravaggio; outstanding among the paintings is a *Madonna and Child* which many believe to be the work of Antonello da Messina, others of Antonio Solario. There are canvases also by Flemish artists, and valuable furnishings, vases and ceramics, some of which are of Eastern origin.

Ibla Archaeological Museum:- Set up during the sixties in rooms under the Hotel Mediterraneo, this museum displays archaeological finds from the province, ordered chronologically and by place.

Section I contains materials pertaining to prehistoric archaeology, from the Paleolithic to the Bronze Age; from this later time are the evidences of the *facies del Castelluccio*.

Section II shows us the findings from the Greek settlement of Camarina, which include many tomb furnishings from the ancient necropolises, clay objects from a fifth-third century B.C. kiln, and Greek and Roman ceramics.

In **Section III** we find the materials from Sicel sites of the Archaic and Classical periods, with particular reference to Monte Casasia, and findings from the necropolises of Rito and Castiglione.

Section IV concentrates on items which have come to light in the Hellenistic sites; we should note the finds from Scornavacche and the faithful reconstruction of a pottery workshop, using the original materials.

In **Section V** materials from the Roman period onward are arranged; of particular interest are the mosaics from an Early Christian place of worship found at Santa Croce Camarina, the finds from Caucana and the inscriptions from Comiso.

Section VI contains finds from various sites.

View of the picturesque town and the eighteenth century
Church of San Giorgio with its spectacular flight of steps.

◄ The Church of San Giuseppe, attributed to R. Gagliardi; and
the balcony of a building in the historical centre.

MODICA

The large town of Modica lies at a short distance from the
capital and can be divided into two different levels, *Modica
Bassa* and *Modica Alta*. A city founded in ancient times, its
origins are probably Greek and Sicel; in Roman times it was
the prosperous *Motyka*, which was then called *Mohac* by the
Arabs, who won possession of it in the ninth century.
The spectacular **Church of San Giorgio** (Cathedral) was originally constructed in the first half of the seventeenth century,
but was entirely rebuilt in the eighteenth century. The magnificent three-tiered facade overlooks an imposing flight of
steps; with its splendid Sicilian Baroque shapes, the exterior
closely resembles the church of the same name in Ragusa.
It was completed, in the upper tier, in the first half of last
century. The interior, a Latin cross in plan, is divided into a
nave and as many as four aisles. In the apse is preserved a
splendid sixteenth century polyptych very probably of the
school of Antonello da Messina.
The **Church of San Pietro** originated in the fourteenth century
but has eighteenth century characteristics, the result of reconstruction after two earthquakes during the seventeenth century. The exquisite two-tiered Baroque facade stands at the top
of a spectacular flight of steps which is bordered by an iron
fence and a number of admirable statues. The aisles, inside,
are divided from the nave by majestic columns with splendid
capitals of Corinthian type.

The excavations of the city of Camarina, which have brought to light a stretch of wall and a temple dedicated to Athena.

The Church of the Madonna delle Grazie and the Theatre of Vittoria.

View toward the island of Capo Passero and a typical salt mine. ►

CAMARINA

The ruins of Camarina lie near the coast and are those of the city founded by the Syracusans in the sixth century B.C. and razed by the Romans in the third century B.C.
The most important vestiges include the **ring walls**, from the period of Timoleon, and the remains of the **Athenaion** (fifth century B.C.), the majestic temple of Athena which must at one time have been extremely impressive. The ruins of houses worth noticing include the **House of the Altar**, the **House of the Inscription** and the **House of the Merchant**.

VITTORIA

A large rural and industrial centre, this town rises on a hill slope overlooking the valley of the Ippari. It is of seventeenth century origin, having been founded by the Colonna and Henriquez families, and its layout and buildings are in eighteenth century style. The **Church of San Giovanni Battista** dates from the early eighteenth century. The powerful three-tiered facade is designed vertically; the interior is of the basilica type with an aisled nave with stucco, marble and gilt adornments. The **Teatro Comunale** (City Theatre) stands out for the sumptuous character of its two-tiered Neo-Classical facade, with ornamental columns and admirable sculptures. The **Church of Santa Maria delle Grazie** is the product of reconstruction in the second half of the eighteenth century.

SYRACUSE

Historical Note:- This city lies on the eastern coast of Sicily, in a charming setting with a picturesque harbour bounded by the Maddalena Peninsula and the island of Ortygia, which is practically connected to the mainland.

Syracuse was one of the most important colonies of Magna Grecia and according to reliable sources was founded by Corinthian settlers in 734 B.C. The first settlements were on the island of Ortygia, which became the original core of a much vaster inhabited area. In Classical times Syracuse was in fact made up of five towns: *Ortygia, Achradina, Tyche, Epipolae* and *Neapolis*. The city grew rapidly in prosperity and military strength, and soon became a magnetic centre of power for the entire Mediterranean basin, defeating the Carthaginians at Hymera (480 B.C.) with the help of Agrigentum. In 474 B.C. the Syracusans, under the command of Hiero, got the better of the Etruscans in the naval battle of Cumae, which placed a limit on the territorial expansion of the latter people toward the south. In 413 B.C. it was the turn of the Athenians to pay the price of opposing the might of Syracuse. Defeated and deported to the Latomie, the great majority of the prisoners met a terrible end.

After various vicissitudes, the city was taken by subterfuge during the Second Punic Wars by the Romans (212 B.C.). When the power of Rome declined, Syracuse suffered repeat-

The eighteenth century facade of the Cathedral.

The little ruined Church of San Giovanni, under which lies the vast fourth to fifth century A.D. necropolis.

The fifth century B.C. Greek theatre, entirely cut out of the rock.

ed attacks by Franks, Vandals and Goths; united with the Byzantine Empire (first half of the sixth century) it housed the court of Constans II, who was assassinated there in 668. Occupied by the Arabs in 878, it lost the important administrative role it had played up to then. In the second half of the eleventh century it was taken over by the Normans, who were followed by the Angevins and, after the events of the Sicilian Vespers, the Aragonese, who brought back to the town its prestige and authority. Under the terms of the Treaty of Utrecht, Syracuse was handed over to the Kingdom of Savoy, and then to the Austrians and Bourbons.

The Syracuse of our time is a city of art and of great archaeological interest, and an outstanding tourist centre, bathing resort and centre for commercial and industrial activities. The city, especially the part on the island of Ortygia, is marked by its clean, white buildings, the beauty of its Medieval and Baroque architecture and the imposing presence of vestiges of its past.

ISLAND OF ORTYGIA

This charming and picturesque islet projects into the natural harbour, dividing the *Porto Grande* from the *Porto Piccolo*. The heart of Syracuse and site of the first Sicel settlements later overlaid by Corinthian colonies, it has several times acted as a refuge and bastion for the people of the entire city.

Cathedral:- The Cathedral rises on the highest point in the island and has a decidedly Baroque character in the eighteenth century facade attributed to A. Palma. The facade overlooks a flight of steps up from the central **Piazza del Duomo**

which is surrounded by other brilliant examples of Baroque architecture. The two-tiered facade is marked by powerful columns and covered in sculptures attributed to Marabitti.

On the site of the Cathedral there rose in ancient times the majestic and sumptuous **Temple of Athena**, a magnificent example of a Doric peripteral structure from the first half of the fifth century B.C. In the Byzantine age, in the seventh century A.D., the temple was transformed into a Christian basilica, as had already been done with the Temple of Concordia at Agrigento. Substantial vestiges of the temple can be seen in the fabric of the church, especially since the additions made in the Baroque age have been eliminated.

The **interior** has the characteristics of a basilica, and is divided into a nave and aisles, with a sixteenth century wooden ceiling in the nave.

Fountain of Arethusa:- This very ancient fresh water spring pours from a cave near the sea, in a setting made evocative by its lush vegetation and by memories associated with the works of Classical authors. Pindar and Virgil take up the tale told by Ibycus in the sixth century B.C.; already at that time he had mentioned this picturesque spring, which according to mythology is the incarnation of the story of Arethusa and Alphaeus and which has also become the symbol of the city.

Temple of Apollo:- At the end of **Piazza Pancali** rise the imposing ruins of this temple building, which were freed during the thirties and forties from the medieval structures that covered them. This is considered to be the oldest of the peripteral Doric temples in Sicily (sixth century B.C.), and was previously erroneously assigned to the cult of Artemis.

137

Archaeological Museum: Sicilian-Italiot vase (fourth century B.C.), depicting Aphrodite in front of a mirror; marble statuette of Hercules (300 B.C.); the sarcophagus of Adelfia (fourth century A.D.) found in the catacombs of San Giovanni.

◄ An evocative view of the Arethusa Fountain.

◄ The powerful ruins of the Temple of Apollo.

THE MAINLAND AND THE ARCHAEOLOGICAL AREA

Many ruins from the Hellenistic and Roman periods can be seen in the area which used to be occupied by the ancient quarters of *Achradina* and *Tyche*.

Roman Gymnasium:- Excavations undertaken in the second half of last century uncovered the remains of a building of the Roman period, improperly identified as a gymnasium. The structure, which dates from the first century A.D., was in all probability a Serapeion, at least during the first stage, before the building was completed. The most important ruins here include the raised *Portico* and the *Theatre*, with a small auditorium facing the stage which also forms one side of the marble *Temple*.

Catacombs of San Giovanni:- This underground cemetery complex belongs to the church of the same name, which the Normans rebuilt on the site of an ancient sixth century basilica and which was ruined by the earthquake of 1693.

Regional Archaeological Museum:- Until recently housed in a building in Piazza Duomo at Ortygia, the Regional Archaeological Museum has been transferred to a very modern building in the **Park of Villa Landolina**, the site of which is a latomia containing some pagan underground tombs of the fourth century B.C. and a Protestant Cemetery where the German Romantic poet A. von Platen is buried. The collections in the museum, one of the most important in Italy from the archaeological point of view, give us a glimpse of Sicel civilization and the various colonies which followed one after another on the island from prehistoric times to the early Christian age.

Greek Theatre:- This impressive theatre building, one of the largest and most evocative that have come down to us from ancient times, is built into the rocky sides of the Temenite Hill, with its auditorium toward the plain of Syracuse and its fringe of sea.

The Theatre goes back originally to the fifth century B.C., having been built by the architect Damocopos. At the time of Hiero II (third century B.C.) the structure underwent considerable remodelling and expanding, which changed its original appearance. Used both for the performance of Classical plays and for public assemblies, the Theatre was the heart of the life of Syracuse from very ancient times. Under the Romans (first to fifth centuries A.D.) the Theatre was further altered to accomodate certain kinds of plays and spectacles typical of the Roman world. Unfortunately the violent plundering of the Theatre in the first half of the sixteenth century, when the upper part of the auditorium and the stage were dismantled to be used as building material in the fortifications of Ortygia, seriously and irrecoverably altered and damaged its structural integrity.

The capacious auditorium, or cavea, which once consisted of 67 tiers of seats, was reduced to 46 tiers divided into nine

View of the auditorium of the Greek theatre.

The Roman amphitheatre, begun in the first century A.D.

The artificial grotto called "Ear of Dionysius".

blocks. In ancient times it was topped by a portico, which collapsed and of which very few vestiges remain; archaeological studies confirm the theory that the *Mouseion* which has provided valuable materials for the city's Archaeological Museum was situated there. In the central part is the *Nymphaeum*, a sort of artificial grotto from which gushed a spring of water, once part of the "plumbing" of the Theatre.

Roman Amphitheatre:- Certainly the largest building of this kind in Sicily, the Amphitheatre dates from the first century B.C. It was built on a grand scale, largely by carving it out of the living rock. Its elliptical plan and structural affinity with the Coliseum confirm that the building was used for circuses and gladiatorial shows.

The **Orecchio di Dionisio** (Ear of Dionysius), as Caravaggio called it, is in the shape of an outer ear and has extraordinary acoustic qualities. Legend recounts that the tyrant of Syracuse shut his enemies in this cave and listened to their conversations from outside.

A view of the necropolis of Grotticelli with the so called "tomb of Archimedes", in reality a Roman columbarium of the first century A.D.

The ara of Hieron II (third century B.C.)

The **Castle of Euryalus**, a powerful fortress, is part of a complex of buildings erected by Dionysius, which included also the walls (fourth century B.C.). The ruins as we see them today are the product of rebuilding in the Byzantine age. The castle rises on the plateau of Epipolae, at a spot considered in ancient times very vulnerable and thus a threat to the safety of Syracuse.

Ara of Hiero II:- This is the biggest altar of Greek antiquity. It was built by Hiero II in the third century B.C. and consists of a rectangular structure measuring 22.8 X 198 metres. In Roman times the pool and portico surrounding it were added. The part cut into the rock has been preserved, while the erected walls were destroyed during the sixteenth century by the Spanish.

The Intagliatella, a stone quarry of the Greek period with rock reliefs; the excavations of Megara Hyblaea.

PALAZZOLO ACREIDE

An important archaeological centre, this town lies up against the spurs of the Hyblaean Hills, in the upper Anapo valley. The modern town was founded in the eighteenth century, near the place where once rose the ancient Syracusan colony of *Akrai*, settled in the seventh century B.C.

On the slopes of the nearby **Acremonte Hill** spread the numerous ruins of the **Archaeological Zone**.

The **Theatre**, discovered in the first half of last century, was built in the third century B.C., and although small is fairly well preserved. The auditorium (partially rebuilt) has twelve tiers of seats in nine blocks.

The **Bouleuterion** stands close by, at the agora, and has six tiers of seats in a semi-circle.

The remains of an archaic temple building (sixth century B.C.) on the site on the **acropolis** provide evidence that a **Temple of Aphrodite** once stood there.

On the south-east slopes of the hill are two stone quarries. The **Latomia dell'Intagliatella** has small niches where little votive panels could have been placed, and a bas-relief carved in the rock with scenes of sacrifices and a banquet. In the nearby **Latomia dell'Intagliata**, hypogea and catacombs of the Early Christian period and cave dwellings from Byzantine times have been found. The **Templi Ferali** are in fact a latomia of similar appearance to the above, where votive and sacrificial objects have been found.

On the the eastern slopes of the Acremonte are the **Santoni**, strange rock carvings of the third century B.C. which spread along a wall of rock and can be connected with the cult of Cybeles.

AUGUSTA

This small town spreads along an island connected by bridges to the mainland, in the upper part of the Gulf of Augusta. The name goes back to the Roman Imperial age, when Augustus founded a new colony here (first century B.C.). Up to two centuries earlier, the Greek colony of *Megara Hyblaea* had existed in this area, but was devastated in conflicts with the Syracusans and Romans. Augusta itself was razed by the Saracens and rebuilt by the Swabians (thirteenth century). Subsequently an Aragonese possession, it suffered badly in more recent times, during the seventeenth and nineteenth centuries, from earthquakes. The locality is also known for an Allied landing there during the last World War (July 1943). A centre of the oil and petrochemical industry, it possesses refineries, factories and a busy commercial port.

The **Castle** goes back to the Swabian period (thirteenth century) and has been used as a prison.

The **Duomo**, originally built in the seventeenth century, had to be rebuilt as a result of the earthquake of 1693 and was completed in the second half of the eighteenth century.

The **Palazzo Comunale** is an elegant seventeenth century building.

The Baroque **Church of the Anime Purganti** (seventeenth century) is also interesting.

The sixteenth century fortalices of **Avalos, Garzia** and **Victoria** can still be seen at the port.

We recommend the excursion to the **ruins of Megara Hyblaea**, which was one of the most ancient Greek colonies in Sicily. The city was founded by Megara (eighth century B.C.) and flourished until its complete destruction by Roman mili-

tia under the command of Marcellus (213 B.C.) It is not easy to understand the layout of the city as restored to us by excavation, since a Hellenistic city was superimposed on an earlier archaic settlement.

An **Antiquarium** exhibits some finds from archaeological studies, but the greater part of the material has been transferred to the museum in the capital.

The ruins easiest to identify include the remains of the **ring walls**, which belong the the Hellenistic period, and the ruins of two turreted structures. The **agora** has been identified; it is surrounded by vestiges of houses of the Hellenistic period, with shops and a courtyard that must have had a wooden colonnade. We can see also traces of very ancient houses, dating from the eighth century B.C. In the upper part of the agora, the point where the **Stoa** (seventh century B.C.) stood has been identified. There are also interesting remains of a **Sanctuary** of the Hellenistic period, of a **Doric temple** probably dedicated to the cult of Aphrodite (fourth century B.C.), of a **Gymnasium** and other temple buildings.

Finally, we should notice the remains of a large **house** of the Hellenistic period, where it is still possible to make out the division of the rooms, and those of a structure used as a bathhouse, with a primitive heating system, later converted by the Romans into a lime kiln.

A view of the city with the eighteenth century Cathedral. ►

The excavations of Megara Hyblaea, a Greek colony of the sixth century B.C.

The auditorium of the Theatre.

CATANIA

Historical Note:- The city spreads along the upper edge of the gulf of the same name, on the Ionian coast of Sicily, in an extremely beautiful natural setting. The mountain of Etna, with its perpetual white cloak of snow, forms a natural backdrop to the city and contrasts strongly with the intense blue of the sky and the yellow of the citrus groves.

The Chalcidian colony of *Catinon* was superimposed on extremely ancient previous settlements, existing in the place since prehistoric times. Subsequently a possession of Geron of Syracuse who called it *Aetna*, it fell again into the hands of its founders (461 B.C.) and was given back its original name. In following centuries the city underwent various vicissitudes connected with the unstable, constantly changing political situation in Sicily at that time.

In the second half of the third century B.C. the Romans made it first a *civitas decumana* and then a true colony, assuring it a period of relative tranquillity.

From the sixth century on it was subjected by Ostrogoths and Byzantines, who were followed by the Arabs. In the eleventh century it passed into the hands of the Normans, who undertook the construction of buildings such as the Cathedral. It was then the turn of the Swabians, followed by the Aragonese, who built the Castello Ursino and made Catania their favourite place of residence.

In 1669 a devastating eruption of Etna covered the city with a thick layer of lava, which reached as far as the sea. Not even thirty years later, in 1693, a catastrophic earthquake completed the ruinous effect of the volcano; the city had to be rebuilt once more, and rose this time with the Baroque character that has lasted up to the present, according to the

designs of G.B.Vaccarini who carried out faithfully the wishes of the Duke of Camastra.

In the nineteenth century Catania took a leading part in the Risorgimento struggles that culminated in the rebellion of Garibaldi. Seriously damaged during the Second World War, the Catania of our days is substantially modern and dynamic in appearance and preserves abundant evidence of its Baroque restoration in the eighteenth century.

The city has a fortunate situation, in a district of increasing importance in the tourist trade, not far from well known resorts on the coast and the volcano of Etna, which besides its interest as a natural phenomenon is acquiring increasing importance as a centre for winter sports and hiking; it also possesses a very active port and is equipped for extensive and diversified commercial, industrial and service activities, to the extent that it may be considered a rival of the regional capital, Palermo.

Duomo:- The Cathedral faces the Piazza Duomo, which provides a refined and harmonious setting. The building was founded in the time of the Norman king Roger I, in the last decade of the eleventh century. Of that original building the back part with three apses and a portion of the transept remain. As early as 1169 a serious earthquake brought down a large part of the Norman structure, which was then rebuilt and again razed by the devastating earthquake of 1693.

The subsequent rebuilding brought into being the Cathedral as we see it today, according to the design of Fra Girolamo Palazzotto which was later completed by the admirable *facade* by G.B.Vaccarini. This facade is one of the masterpieces

Piazza del Duomo: the Cathedral, the Municipal Palace and the Fountain of the Elephant.

The "Teatro Bellini", inaugurated in 1890, and the imposing ▶ mass of the "Castello Ursino", built by Frederick II of Swabia in 1239-1250.

of the Baroque style in Sicily; it was built in the first half of the eighteenth century and has two tiers of columns, of which those on the ground floor are very ancient and probably belonged to an earlier building. The imposing *interior*, which is divided into a nave and two aisles, offers us an exceptionally fascinating ambience, deriving from the combination of elements of the original Norman architecture with the Baroque reconstruction superimposed on them. The transept, which survives from the first Norman building, has at its ends two incomplete bell towers, while over its centre rises the cupola of Battaglia. By the second pilaster on the right is the *tomb of Vincenzo Bellini* (1810-1835), one of the most illustrious sons of the city. In the right apse is the *Chapel of St.Agatha*, which is enclosed by an exquisite wrought-iron railing. We can admire there the *Funerary monument of the Viceroy Ferdinando d'Acuña*, a very fine work by the sculptor Antonello Freri.

Church of San Nicolò:- This eighteenth century church is one of the largest religious buildings in Sicily, and is characterized by its powerful *facade*, which remained incomplete and is adorned with immense truncated columns. Especially striking is the crowning of the central portion of the facade, which is of dark lava rock that contrasts with the clean white of the wall. The *interior*, of imposing dimensions, is divided into a nave and aisles by impressive pillars, and is marked by sober lines and the complete absence of decorative features. In the floor of the transept is a curious *sundial* with the signs of the zodiac, the work of Bertel Thorwaldsen (first half of the nineteenth century).

Porta Uzeda:- This structure from the end of the seventeenth century, Baroque in appearance, stands at the beginning of the *Via Etnea*, the lively centre of the city, its main street, lined with architecturally fine buildings, and the meeting place of the citizens of Catania.
Close by, overlooking the port, is the *Palazzo dell'Arcivescovado* (Archbishop's Palace), with the *Palazzo Biscari*.

Palazzo del Municipio:- The City Hall faces the *Piazza del Duomo*, where we can see the *Fountain of the Elephant*, an eighteenth century work by G.B.Vaccarini who composed it by standing an Egyptian obelisk on an ancient elephant in lava rock of the Roman period; this image has become the emblem of the city of Catania. Known in popular idiom as *Liotru*, it was restored by Vaccarini himself after being damaged in the earthquake of 1693. The *Palazzo del Municipio* was built by Vaccarini in the first half of the eighteenth century and is marked by admirable architectural forms. We should observe the ashlarwork on the ground floor, the arrangement of the pilasters, the balconied windows on the upper floor, and the central portal flanked by twin columns which support the balustrade of the middle balcony.

Castello Ursino:- This powerful square castle was built in the first half of the thirteenth century by Riccardo da Lentini, who designed it for Frederick II of Swabia. The king wanted it to defend his coastline from the danger of pirate raids as well as to provide him with a fortress in the city from which he could control possible popular insurrections. The castle was

The Fountain of the Elephant by G.B. Vaccarini (1736); two views of Piazza Stesicoro with the remains of the Roman amphitheatre, probably of the second century A.D.

remodelled in the sixteenth century and restored after the damage it suffered in the eruption of Etna in 1669.

Roman Theatre:- The easily recognizable remains of this Roman theatre building go back to the Imperial period, when it was erected on the site of an ancient Greek theatre of the fifth century B.C. It is reached by way of the door to the building of the *Soprintendenza alle Belle Arti* (Via Vittorio Emanuele 266). We can admire the central portion of the auditorium, the ambulatories and the remains of the orchestra with its marble floor.
Immediately adjacent are the remains of the **Odeon**, a sort of smaller theatre where the members of the chorus rehearsed.

Roman Amphitheatre:- The amphitheatre stands at the edge of Piazza Stesicoro, and is an important example of Roman public building. The imposing elliptical structure was only slightly smaller than the Coliseum in Rome. It dates from the second century A.D.; it seems it was able to seat up to 16,000 spectators. Decaying and ruined from the fifth century onward, it became a quarry for materials for new public works. On the square, at the end of which stands the facade of the **Church of the Cappuccini**, we find also the **Monument to Bellini** erected in the second half of last century by G. Monteverde.

Teatro Bellini:- This theatre is a building in Classical style of the second half of last century, named after the great composer from Catania. It is the work of the architects A.Scala and C.Sada, and is distinguished by its splendid auditorium.

ACI CASTELLO - ACI TREZZA

Aci Castello is the first important centre on the picturesque *Riviera dei Ciclopi*, which lies to the north of Catania and the population of which has lived for centuries by fishing, using even now their traditional methods. In relatively recent times the locality has undergone considerable development as a summer bathing and holiday resort, while in the surrounding countryside intensive citrus cultivation prospers. In the second half of the twelfth century the town was razed by a disastrous earthquake, which forced the population to take refuge in neighbouring localities; developing as centres, these places preserved in their names the recognizable prefix "Aci".

The distinctive feature of Aci Castello is, precisely, the **Castle**; founded by the Normans and built on top of a dark basalt rock in the second half of the eleventh century; it is memorable for its situation sheer above the sea.

The nearby town of **Aci Trezza** is known as the scene of the events in Giovanni Verga's famous novel *I Malavoglia*. It is also a popular bathing resort in a very charming natural setting. A few hundred metres from the shore the basalt shapes of the **faraglioni** or "Scogli dei Ciclopi" (Rocks of the Cyclops) rise from the sea; according to tradition, these rocks are the huge stones that the giant Polyphemus threw at Ulysses.

The largest of these rocks, once known as the *Island of Lachea*, was donated by a private citizen to the University of Catania, which has installed there a marine physics and biology research station.

Two views of the picturesque coast of Aci Castello and the nearby Aci Trezza.

Piazza del Duomo: the eighteenth century Cathedral and to the right of it the seventeenth century Basilica of Santi Pietro e Paolo.

The sumptuous Baroque facade of the Church of San Sebastiano.

(Right), two views of Etna erupting. Next pages, Etna with ▶ snow on it and the coast of Giardini-Naxos; eruption and lava flow at night; the amazing flora on the slopes of the volcano.

ACIREALE

This town stands on a terraced slope of volcanic origin between the last spurs of Etna and the Ionian coast. Its fame comes from its thermal springs, also of volcanic origin, which have given rise to modern spas.

The **Duomo** dates from the sixteenth to seventeenth centuries, but was remodelled in the eighteenth century. The seventeenth century facade is the work of G.B.Basile and is marked by a fine portal in marble alabaster (seventeenth century). The majestic interior has its crossing and choir richly decorated in frescoes, the work of eighteenth century artists (P.P.Vasta, A.Filocamo).

In the Piazza del Duomo, the centre of the town, we find also the **Palazzo Comunale**, of the second half of the seventeenth century, in typical Catanese Baroque style, and the **Church of Santi Pietro e Paolo**, a seventeenth century building with the characteristics of a basilica, the distinguishing features of which are the lively lines of the facade, a splendid piece of architecture on two tiers crowned by ornaments; the elegant columns that divide up its space are of twin design on the inside.

We should not neglect to visit the **Villa Belvedere**, the public gardens, which offer us an admirable panoramic view of Etna and the sea. A pleasant walk through an impressive and beautiful landscape along the steep slopes of the "Timpa" takes us to the pleasant fishing village of **Santa Maria la Scala**.

ETNA

Mount Etna, which is 3343 metres high, is the tallest active volcano in the continent of Europe. Because of its great importance to the natural sciences, its exceptionally beautiful landscape and its human and ecological interest, the Etna district has recently been declared, with the proper legislative backing of the Region of Sicily, a National Park.

The highest part of the volcano has also attracted tourists interested in snow sports, and adequate facilities for the practise of the most popular winter sports have been provided. This imposing volcanic mass, whose huge cone dominates the north-eastern section of the island, has since very ancient times played an active part in the island's life and been surrounded by myths and legends. Known also as *Mongibello*, a name of ancient Arab origin, it is marked by the great variety of species of trees and plants that clothe its sides and change as its altitude increases, making way finally for a landscape of desert character. The many eruptions which have occurred over the centuries have often altered the profile of Etna, forming new vents, pushing up new cones, and profoundly altering also the contours of the local orographic structure and its morphological features.

Of the innumerable eruptions that have occurred (at least 135 have been counted in historical times), one of the most disastrous was that of 1669, which had terrible consequences for nearby Catania. In this century there have been frequent eruptions, some of which have been extremely serious and caused considerable damage and waste in the Etna district. One of the most recent and spectacular eruptions, in Spring 1983, made it necessary to use explosives to deviate in a safe direction the immense streams of lava which were threatening villages on the slopes of the volcano.

One of the classical itineraries for a visit to the volcano branches off at Catania on the **Nicolosi** road as far as the Canto-

View of the town and the Gothic Church of Santa Maria.

niera dell'Etna; from here it is possible to visit the spectacular crater, with the help of expert guides and carefully respecting elementary rules of caution and common sense. The top of the crater can be extremely dangerous, because the volcano may throw up pyroclastic material, sometimes unexpectedly. A trip particularly worth taking uses as a base the **Sapienza Refuge** (1910 metres), which makes it possible to walk right round the volcano, passing by interesting villages and admiring one of the most distinctive landscapes in Sicily.

RANDAZZO

This town is situated near the meeting of the Alcantara and Flascio rivers, in the valley between the volcanic massif of Etna and the Nebrodi-Peloritani mountain chain. The layout of the town reveals its medieval origin; it has many buildings in volcanic stone, and goes back to the Byzantine period, having grown up on the site of an ancient Sicel settlement. It prospered particularly under the Aragonese.
The **Church of San Nicolò** is of fourteenth century origin; the fabric of the apse is of that period. The building as we see it today is the result of alterations in the sixteenth and seventeenth centuries; it contains important sculptures by Gagini. The **Church of Santa Maria** is from the thirteenth century; the original three apses of the building still stand. The portals at the sides possess fifteenth century Catalan features, while the facade and the bell tower, in their final version, date from alterations made in the second half of last century. The interior has an aisled nave and is adorned by sixteenth to eighteenth century paintings and sculptures from the workshop of the Gagini, including a polygonal shrine and the baptismal font.

Three views of the fascinating Alcantara Gorge.

THE ALCANTARA GORGE

The Alcantara gorge, an absolute must for tourists visiting the area, can be reached from Taormina-Giardini Naxos by following the main road inland (185) towards Francavilla di Sicilia for 13 kilometres.

This natural monument of basalt rock was created by the eruption of the volcano Monte Moio, Etna's most eccentric offshoot, around the year 2400 BC. The lava flow invaded the entire valley of the Alcantara river as far as its mouth on the coast, where the Greeks founded their first colony in Sicily.

In the Sciara Larderia region the river of lava reached a thickness of 70 metres. While still white-hot, and due to a telluric settling, a sinuous longitudinal crack opened in the lava over a length of 500 metres, 70 metres deep and five metres wide, thus assuming the appearance of a gorge. Only later, all the waters of the catchment basin feeding the Alcantara river flowed into the fissure and from this derived the name "Alcantara gorge". The continous action of the water smoothed the basalt walls of the gorge producing that gleaùing lustre which can be admired only under the action of light.

The gorge is reached by way of a scenic footpath or by means of modern elevators. To reach the entrance of the gorge the use of wading boots is recommended, which can be hired at the site; these are a useful protection against the icy water and spiky rocks.

The gorge is always a dangerous place for non-experts and those who are unfamiliar with the site.

There is a large car-park, a bar, a restaurant and farm holiday facilities; it is possible to stay the night, and taste and buy excellent food prepared with traditional recipes.

A charming view of the town.

Two views of the Greek-Roman theatre, begun in the ►
third century B.C.

TAORMINA

Almost at the border of the province of Catania lies Taormina, on the slopes of Mount Tauro, in a very charming and panoramic spot that makes it one of the chief glories of Sicily. Because of its particularly fortunate micro-climate and its splendid natural situation, on a hill terrace overlooking the Ionian coast with the majestic and spectacular Etna as a backdrop, and owing also to the vastness of its historical, cultural and archaeological heritage, it is one of the places most visited by tourists in the whole island, a winter resort and a very important centre for holidaying. The town possesses refined and practical hotel and lodging facilties, extending to the beaches of **Isola Bella, Mazzarò** and **Spisone**, which are connected to the centre also by a cable car.

Greek in origin, *Tauromenion* grew up in the fourth century B.C. as a result of the decline of the Chalcidian colony of Naxos, even if it seems certain that when the first centre was founded Sicels were also present. It soon became part of the sphere of influence of Syracuse, and remained faithful to that city until the first Roman colonization, around the third century B.C. When Syracuse declined, Taormina became the capital of Byzantine Sicily, up to the time of the Arab conquest, at the beginning of the tenth century; it subsequently recovered its prosperity under the Normans.

The **Greek Theatre** is without question the most important feature for sight-seers, also because of its very fortunate natural setting, with splendid views toward the Calabrian coast, the Ionian coast of Sicily and the spectacular volcanic cone of Etna. The Theatre as we find it today is undoubtedly of the Roman period (second century B.C.); it was superimposed on earlier, similar structures of the Hellenistic period. The ancient Greek origins of the complex are evidenced by some inscriptions on the steps and the remains of a little temple which was sacrificed by the Romans when they enlarged the auditorium.

Adjacent to the Theatre is the **Antiquarium** where archaeological finds of great interest are exhibited: there are epigraphs and sculptures, among the latter a *torso* copying a Greek original, a *woman's head* in marble of the Hellenistic period and a sarcophagus of the same material.

The remains of **Baths** of the Imperial period, consisting of three large rooms and several smaller ones, have come to light on the site of the ancient **Forum**, which is the present Piazza Vittorio Emanuele.

The **Naumachia** was probably a monumental nymphaeum built in the Imperial age, when the city was enriched by many public works. The present appearance of this structure is a wall with large apsed niches and a cistern behind it in a very poor state of repair.

Lastly, the vestiges of ancient Taormina include the **Odeon**, a covered theatre of the Imperial period, dating from the second century A.D. The auditorium, which is built of brick, consists of five small blocks, while the stage is backed by an

ancient temple, partially incorporated into the Church of Santa Caterina, built much later; it is still not known to what god the temple was dedicated.

The **Palazzo Corvaja** is a fifteenth century building constructed for the meetings of the first parliament on the island. It has a battlemented facade enhanced by lancet windows and a fine portal in Catalan Gothic style; there is a Latin inscription on the cornice. The small courtyard is charming.

The **Duomo** was originally built in the thirteenth century, but substantially altered during the Renaissance. The simple facade, which has three sections, is topped by a battlemented crowning. On the right side is a portal of Gothic appearance (sixteenth century), while the left side has a fifteenth century portal. The interior is divided into a nave and two aisles by large columns supporting ogival arches.

In front of the building is a seventeenth century **fountain** in Baroque style with mythological figures, which is the emblem of the city. The busy main street is the **Corso Umberto**, which provides a lively promenade for tourists and is lined with elegant shops and restaurants. Following this street we come to the scenic Piazza 9 Aprile, where the former **Church of Sant'Agostino**, a Gothic building of the fifteenth century, still stands; further on is the **Torre dell'Orologio** (Clock Tower), with a gate in it (**Porta di Mezzo**)leading to an area of great architectural and artistic interest, with many typically medieval features.

The **Badia Vecchia**, known also as *Badiazza*, is an evocative building in the form of a tower rising above the houses of the town. Built in the fifteenth century, it is a pleasing, square

Regional Museum: a sixteenth century work by an unknown follower of Laurana from Messina; a marble Madonna and Child, *attributed to Laurana;* St. Catherine of Alessandria, *a sixteenth century work.*

The snowy peak of Etna as a backdrop to the Greek theatre ►
in Taormina.

building which has been considerably restored. It is crowned by Ghibelline battlements, below which is a series of very fine ogival lancet windows; in the upper part they rest on a band of lava rock and pumice inlays.

The **Palazzo Ciampoli** goes back to the first half of the fifteenth century and is in typically Catalan Gothic style; the facade is lightened by a row of elegant lancet windows.

The **Palazzo of the Dukes of Santo Stefano** was the home of the De Spuches family. The fourteenth to fifteenth century building has stylistic similarities to the Badia Vecchia and is marked by the rows of decorative lancet windows on the second floor, while the first floor has small trefoil arches. We should notice the decorative strip that completes the building at the top, made of lava rock and pumice inlay.

A characteristic feature of Taormina is the **Albergo San Domenico**, a hotel in a converted monastery building, of which the pleasant sixteenth century cloister and some of the interior decorations remain. Of the adjacent church of the same name, which was ruined by bombing in the Second World War, only the Baroque bell tower (sixteenth century) has been preserved.

Just outside the **Porta Messina** is the small **Church of San Pancrazio**, below which substantial remains of a Hellenistic temple have been found. Some inscriptions found inside it support the theory that it was dedicated to the cult of Isis and Serapis.

A pleasant walk along a track with fine views leads to the powerful medieval **Castle**, built at the top of Mount Tauro where the ancient acropolis once rose. From the top of the castle we can admire a wide and beautiful view.

Piazza del Duomo, with the fourteenth century Cathedral of San Nicola and the beautiful fountain, 1635; the entrance to Palazzo Corvaja (early fifteenth century) and the facade of the elegant Palazzo of the Dukes of Santo Stefano (fourteenth and fifteenth centuries).

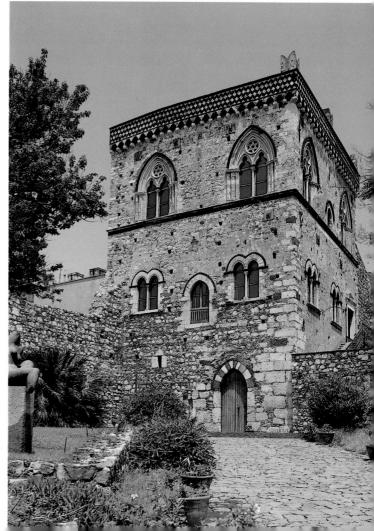

The battlemented tower of the "Badia Vecchia" (fourteenth centruy); the picturesque steps of San Francesco di Luna.

163

GIARDINI NAXOS

The most important sea resorts of this part of the Ionian coast include **Letojanni**, the already mentioned **Mazzarò**, with its beautiful sickle-shaped beach, and above all **Giardini-Naxos**. This last is an enchanting seasonal and bathing resort with excellent tourist facilities, which has developed on the site of the ancient Greek colony of *Naxos*, founded in the eighth century B.C. and destroyed by the Syracusans three centuries later. What remains of the ancient settlement are substantial vestiges of the **walls**, dating from the sixth century B.C., some **gates** and a **tower**, besides the space that must have been occupied by a vast **sanctuary**. In this large area an ancient temple probably dedicated to the cult of Aphrodite has been identified (seventh to fifth centuries B.C.). Also in this area an **altar** and two **kilns**, probably connected with the sanctuary, have come to light. Another section of the archaeological area is occupied by the ruins of the city built to replace the one destroyed in 476 B.C.; remains of **temples** and artisans' **workshops** (those of makers of clay vases and statues) have been found here. The numerous finds from the area (pottery, clay objects, sculptures, terracottas, architectural fragments) are displayed in the **Archaeological Museum of Naxos**, which is situated in the former Bourbon Fort on Cape Schisò.

Four views of the sunny locality of Giardini-Naxos: the little port; the incomparable beauty of the coast; the dark shape of smoking Etna in the background; the modern baths.

MESSINA

Historical Note:- This city, known as the *"Gateway to Sicily"* lies under the foothills of the Peloritani mountains, facing the strait of Messina, which takes its name from the city and is the umbilical cord joining Sicily to the continent. Called *Zancle* by the natives of the island because of the sickle shape of its natural harbour, it was settled by Chalcidian peoples as far back as the eighth century B.C. Later a possession of Anaxilas of Rhegium, it was populated by Messenian colonists who gave it the name of *Messana*. In the centuries that followed, the city was the cause of fierce disputes between Doric and Ionian peoples, and was involved in the conflicts between the Sicilian cities which culminated in the victory of Hannibal and the Carthaginian occupation. In 264 B.C. the Romans intervened, freeing the city from the Carthaginians and making it into a bridgehead for further conquests in the island. The new *civitas foederata* then enjoyed a long period of prosperity and well-being, forming a sort of "happy island" in the midst of the troubled scene presented by the rest of Sicily, which suffered plundering, death and devastation under Verres and in the war of the slaves.

After the fall of the empire the city was occupied by Goths and Byzantines, who held it for a long time, up until the coming of the Muslims (ninth century). In the eleventh century the city, which was impatient under Arab rule, welcomed the Norman invaders, who made it into an important local capital. Subsequently subjected to Swabian rule, it could not tolerate the loss of its independence, which gave rise to an im-

pulsive revolt (first half of the thirteenth century). Messina was then taken over by the Angevins (except that it fought them at the time of the "Vespers"); becoming Aragonese, it followed the fortunes of the Spanish house, although with brief interruptions, until the eighteenth century. On the coming of the Savoys, Bourbons and Austrians during the first three decades of the eighteenth century, it fell into the sphere of the Bourbons (1734), who ruled it until Sicily was annexed to the Kingdom of Italy in 1860. The city lies in an area with a high earthquake risk, and has often suffered earthquakes. Among those in relatively recent times we will mention the one on February 5th 1783, which razed it to the ground, and the catastrophic one on 18th December 1908, which was followed by a tidal wave and almost wiped Messina from the face of the earth, claiming not less than 80,000 victims in the city alone. As if that was not enough, the Second World War inflicted more hard blows on the already mutilated city.

Messina, as we see it today, is a fine modern city, restored to its former splendour by a grid of wide, well-lit avenues, lined by buildings which are strictly earthquake-resistant, in the context of an extremely symmetrical and linear city layout. Although very little remains of its architectural wonders and the considerable ruins that existed of its very ancient past, it is a city of great interest for its art and is surrounded by a region of great natural beauty. It is a magnetic commercial centre and an important port for traffic between Sicily and the rest of Italy.

Piazza del Duomo seen from above, and the facade of the Cathedral which still preserves the sobriety of its medieval origins.

◄ A view of the Strait.

Duomo:- The present appearance of the splendid Cathedral is the result of relatively recent rebuilding after the severe damage it suffered during the bombing of 1943; the church had already been rebuilt after the earthquake of 1908. The imposing building, flanked by a powerful and elegant bell tower, looks on to the Piazza Duomo where the Fountain of Orion stands. The original church was built in the second half of the twelfth century by the Norman king Roger II, replacing a previous Medieval building.

Of the *facade*, the only part belonging to the original building is the lower portion with inlays in relief representing scenes of ethnographical and historical interest. The rich and elegant portals are Gothic and the middle one, crowned by a tall carved spire, has at both sides lions supporting on their backs fine spiral columns. The side doors are from the sixteenth century, while the triple apse is quite impressive.

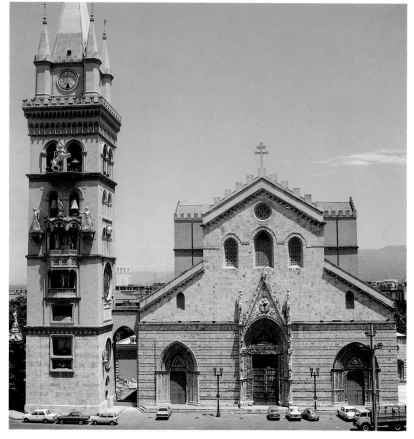

The **interior** has the form of a basilica with the nave divided from the aisles by columns supporting ogival arches. Almost entirely rebuilt, it has a wooden ceiling with original designs. Of great interest is the **Treasury**, which has been arranged in showcases and consists of fourteenth to seventeenth century chalices, twelfth to seventeenth century reliquiaries, eighteenth century bronze candelabra, valuable embroideries in gold and silver (seventeenth century), silk copes and chasubles (eighteenth century), rings, seals, rich mitres, illumined chorals, silver vases (seventeenth-eighteenth centuries), paintings from the Byzantine age and other valuable objects and furnishings. A story in itself is the very unusual **Bell tower**, several times ruined by earthquakes and rebuilt according to the original Norman model. It is topped by a spire with four pinnacles around it and possesses an admirable clockwork mechanism commissioned by Bishop Paino and inaugurated in 1933. Its unusual moving figures represent subjects connected with religion, astronomy and local history.

Church of the Santissima Annunziata dei Catalani:- This church was originally built in the Norman period, in the second half of the twelfth century, but it was remodelled in the following century. The cupola, transept and apse of the present building preserve the original structures. The **facade** goes back to the thirteenth century and has a central portal in the shape of an arch, with other portals to the sides each crowned by an architrave and a lancet window. The church, which was used as a royal chapel in the time of the Aragonese, was later used as a foundlings' hospital. In the sixteenth century it became a Dominican church and later accomoda-

The sixteenth century Fountain of Orion, the work of G.A. Montorsoli, and the Church of the Santissima Annunziata dei Catalani, begun in the twelfth century.

The facade and the apse of the Church of San Francesco;
below, the votive church of Cristo Re.

ted a confraternity of Catalan merchants, which gave it its name. The ***interior*** has an aisled nave divided by columns with
a barrel and cross vault, and reveals a mixture of influences,
Arab, Roman and Lombard.

Church of San Francesco d'Assisi:- Among the finest religious
buildings in Messina, this church was seriously damaged by
a fire in the second half of last century and almost completely
razed by the disastrous earthquake of 1908. However, in
spite of repeated alterations over the centuries, the church
still retains the appearance of a thirteenth century building.
The original church was built in Norman times, with Sicilian-
Arab features. We are surprised by the elegant and impressive
exterior of the triple apse with its unusual crowning of
Guelph battlements. On the right side is an ogival portal remaining from the original building.

Fountain of Orion:- This is a masterpiece by the Florentine
artist Fra Giovanni Angelo da Montorsoli (sixteenth century);
the admirable statue of the mythical founder of the city stands
at the top of a pedestal formed by two basins separated and
supported by mythological figures, which rises from a larger,
polygonal basin enlivened by statues and allegorical
representations of the *Tiber*, the *Nile*, the *Ebro* and the
Camaro.

Regional Museum:- The museum is in the rooms of what
used to be the *Mellingoff Spinning Mill*, and contains interesting archaeological, medieval and modern art exhibits.

An evocative aerial view of the sanctuary of the Black Madonna, and the typical tongues of golden sand round Tindari.

TINDARI

Tindari is an area of great archaeological interest at the western end of the bay between Cape Tindari and the Cape of Milazzo. Founded in the first half of the fourth century B.C. to celebrate the victory of the Syracusans over Carthage, it was known as *Tyndaris*, and was a loyal ally first of its mother city and then, from the third century B.C., of Rome, which it always supported in its long military struggle with Carthage. In the Imperial age it became the *Colonia Augusta Tyndaritanorum*, and later suffered recurrent natural disasters, landslides and earthquakes, which led to a relentless decline culminating its its destruction at the hand of the Arabs.

We can still see substantial remains of the **walls**, some sections of which are the original city walls, while other portions are of later date. The outstanding feature of the ruins is the **Greek Theatre**, which dates from the fourth century B.C., and where excavation and restoration were begun in the first half of last century. Near a vaulted structure, improperly supposed to be a basilica but almost certainly a monumental entrance porch, is a vast block of buildings on several levels, known as **Isolato IV**. The lower levels are occupied by the remains of Roman houses and shops *(tabernae)*. The upper level consists of the remains of the **Baths**, dating from the second century A.D.

In the **Museum** beside the Theatre we can see some interesting finds from the excavations.

In modern Tindari, which probably grew up on the site of the ancient *agora*, we should visit the **Santuario**, a modern building rising on the site of the acropolis of the ancient settlement, near a smaller sixteenth century sanctuary now out of bounds to the public.

MILAZZO

This town rises at the eastern end of the gulf of the same name, at the base of a peninsula projecting into the waters of the Tyrrhenian sea. Archaeological finds provide proof that the area was first settled by humans in extremely ancient times; there are traces of necropolises dating from the fourteenth century B.C. Because of its strategic importance, the town was always a centre of military interest. A town was built on the present site around the eighth century B.C. by the Chalcidians (there had already been Sicel settlements there), as a stronghold for Messina. Near this ancient town of *Mylae*, the Carthaginians were defeated by the Romans in a naval battle in the third century B.C.; subsequently Sextus Pompeius was defeated there during the civil war. An important administrative centre during the Arab and Norman ages, the town retained its powers under the Spanish also. In 1860 Garibaldi won an important victory over the Bourbons there, during his memorable campaign.

The **Castle** in its present form goes back to the fifteenth to sixteenth centuries, when the Spanish further fortified the previous thirteenth century structure built by Frederick II of Swabia. In the highest part of the town, near the castle and the ring walls, stands the **Duomo Vecchio** (Old Cathedral), a seventeenth century building in Renaissance style. The **Church (Sanctuary) of San Francesco di Paola** contains a fine Madonna and Child by Gagini.

In the **Duomo Nuovo** (New Cathedral) are preserved interesting paintings by the sixteenth century artist Antonello de Saliba. We should also see the Gothic **Palazzo dei Giudici** and the **Palazzo Municipale** which contains mementos of the Risorgimento, a well-stocked library and various paintings.

The narrow strip of land on which Milazzo lies.

A view of the gigantic rocks of Panarea, the pearl of the Aeolian islands.

Next page, Lipari, the biggest island in the archipelago, and the wonderful harsh landscape of Vulcano.

AEOLIAN ISLANDS

The Aeolian archipelago (Alicudi, Filicudi, Lipari, Panarea, Salina, Stromboli and Vulcano) lies off the coast of Milazzo and is made up of seven major islands and a series of rocks and islets. The main geological component of these islands is volcanic rock and lava from several quite separate eras; the result is wild coasts with sheer cliffs above the sea, a landscape of fascinating beauty enhanced by innumerable small craters and still active volcanos.

The first settlements on the island date from prehistoric times. Around 4000 B.C. Neolithic peoples settled on Lipari. There is evidence that as early as the eighteenth century B.C. Aeolian peoples had established there bases on the important trade routes passing through the Straits of Messina. The flourishing Aeolian civilization declined because of a sudden depopulation around the tenth century B.C. Toward the sixth century B.C. Greek colonizers of Doric extraction repopulated the archipelago; at the time of the Punic Wars (third century B.C.) it became a strategic stronghold for the Carthaginians, and a fierce battle occurred in its waters between the Carthaginians and Romans (257 B.C.).

In the early Middle Ages Lipari was a bishops' see and a religious centre of great importance. It revived in the Norman period, thanks to a community of Benedictine monks, and from then on shared the fortunes of Sicily and the Kingdom of Naples.

INDEX

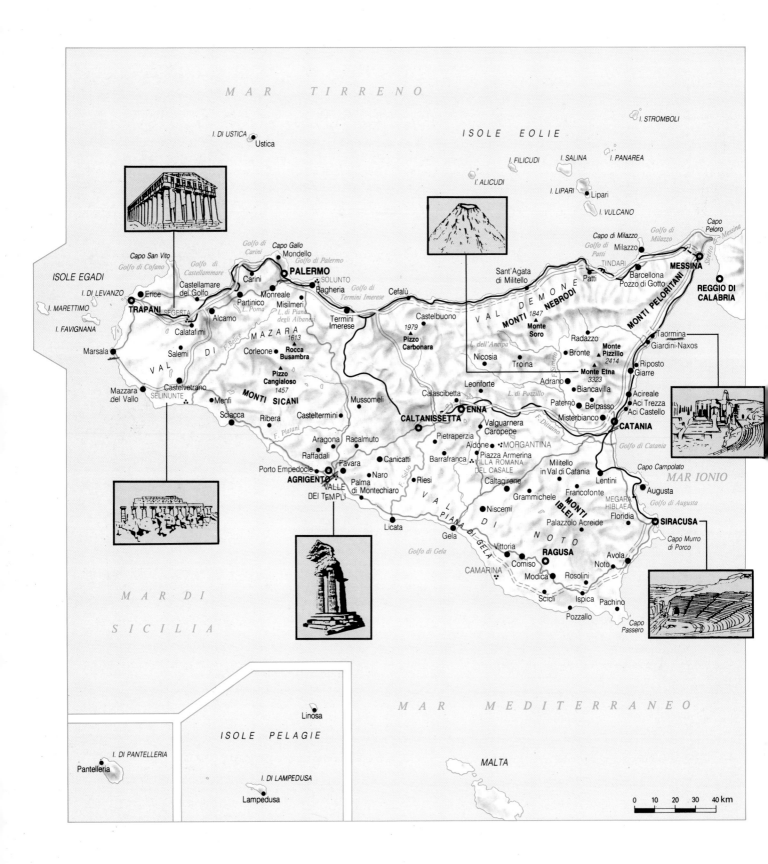

MAR TIRRENO

ISOLE EOLIE

I. STROMBOLI

I. DI USTICA
Ustica

I. FILICUDI
I. SALINA
I. PANAREA

I. ALICUDI

I. LIPARI
Lipari
I. VULCANO

Capo Peloro
Stretto di Messina

ISOLE EGADI

Capo San Vito
Golfo di Cofano
Golfo di Castellammare
Golfo di Carini
Capo Gallo
Mondello
Golfo di Palermo

Capo di Milazzo
Golfo di Milazzo
Milazzo
Golfo di Patti

Capo di Milazzo

MESSINA

I. DI LEVANZO
Erice
Castellamare del Golfo
Carini
PALERMO
SOLUNTO
Bagheria
Golfo di Termini Imerese
Cefalù

Sant'Agata di Militello
Patti
TINDARI
Barcellona
Pozzo di Gotto

REGGIO DI CALABRIA

I. MARETTIMO

TRAPANI
SEGESTA
Partinico
Monreale
Misilmeri
L. di Piana degli Albanesi
Termini Imerese

VAL DEMONE
MONTI NEBRODI
Monte Soro
1847
Radazzo

MONTI PELORITANI
Taormina

I. FAVIGNANA

Alcamo
Calatafimi
MAZARA
1613
Rocca Busambra
L. Poma

Castelbuono
1979
Pizzo Carbonara

L. dell'Ancipa
Nicosia
Troina

Bronte
Monte Pizzillo
2414

Giardini-Naxos
Riposto
Giarre

Marsala
Salemi
VAL
DI
Corleone
Pizzo Cangialoso
1457
MONTI SICANI

Leonforte
Calascibetta
L. di Pozzillo

Adrano
Monte Etna
3323
Biancavilla
Paternò

Acireale
Aci Trezza
Aci Castello

Mazzara del Vallo
Castelvetrano
SELINUNTE
Menfi
Sciacca
Ribera

Castelltermini
Mussomeli

ENNA
CALTANISSETTA
Valguarnera
Caropepe
Pietraperzia
Aidone
MORGANTINA

Belpasso
Misterbianco
CATANIA

Golfo di Catania

Aragona
Racalmuto
Raffadali
Favara
Canicatti

Barrafranca
Piazza Armerina
VILLA ROMANA
DEL CASALE

Militello in Val di Catania
Lentini

Capo Campolato

MAR IONIO

Porto Empedocle
AGRIGENTO
VALLE DEI TEMPLI
Naro
Palma di Montechiaro
Riesi

Caltagirone
Grammichele
Francofonte

MEGARA
HIBLAEA
Augusta
Golfo di Augusta

MAR DI

SICILIA

Licata

VAL DI PIANA DI GELA

Niscemi

MONTI
IBLEI
Palazzolo Acreide

Floridia

SIRACUSA

Capo Murro di Porco

Gela
Golfo di Gela
CAMARINA

NOTO
Vittoria
RAGUSA
Comiso
Modica
Scicli
Ispica
Pozzallo

Avola
Noto
Rosolini
Pachino

Capo Passero

MAR MEDITERRANEO

Linosa

ISOLE PELAGIE

I. DI PANTELLERIA
Pantelleria

I. DI LAMPEDUSA
Lampedusa

MALTA

0 10 20 30 40 km